Social Movement

Key Concepts in Political Science

GENERAL EDITOR: Leonard Schapiro

EXECUTIVE EDITOR: Peter Calvert

Other titles in the same series include:

ALREADY PUBLISHED

Martin Albrow	**Bureaucracy**
Peter Calvert	**Revolution**
Brian Chapman	**Police State**
Ioan Davies	**Social Mobility and Political Change**
Joseph Frankel	**National Interest**
John Plamenatz	**Ideology**
Paul Wilkinson	**Social Movement**

IN PREPARATION

Shlomo Avineri	**Utopianism**
Stanley Benn	**Power**
Anthony H. Birch	**Representation**
Karl Deutsch	**Legitimacy**
S. E. Finer	**Dictatorship**
C. J. Friedrich	**Tradition and Authority**
Geoffrey Goodwin	**International Society**
Julius Gould	**Violence**
E. Kamenka and Alice Erh-Soon Tay	**Law**
J. F. Lively	**Democracy**
Robert Orr	**Liberty**
John C. Rees	**Equality**
Leonard Schapiro	**Totalitarianism**
Henry Tudor	**Political Myth**

Social Movement

Paul Wilkinson
University College, Cardiff

Macmillan

First published in 1971 by Pall Mall Press Ltd

Published by The Macmillan Press Ltd
London and Basingstoke.
Associated companies in New York Toronto Dublin
Melbourne Johannesburg and Madras

SBN (paper) 333 11788 3

Printed in Great Britain by
The Pitman Press, Bath

Not for sale in the U.S.A.

Contents

'Key Concepts' an Introductory Note

Political concepts are part of our daily speech—we abuse 'bureaucracy' and praise 'democracy', welcome or recoil from 'revolution'. Emotive words such as 'equality', 'dictatorship', 'élite' or even 'power' can often, by the very passions which they raise, obscure a proper understanding of the sense in which they are, or should be, or should not be, or have been used. Confucius regarded the 'rectification of names' as the first task of government. 'If names are not correct, language will not be in accordance with the truth of things', and this in time would lead to the end of justice, to anarchy and to war. One could with some truth point out that the attempts hitherto by governments to enforce their own quaint meanings on words have not been conspicuous for their success in the advancement of justice. 'Rectification of names' there must certainly be: but most of us would prefer such rectification to take place in the free debate of the university, in the competitive arena of the pages of the book or journal.

Analysis of commonly used political terms, their reassessment or their 'rectification', is, of course, normal activity in the political science departments of our universities. The idea of this series was indeed born in the course of discussion between a few university teachers of political science, of whom Professor S. E. Finer of Manchester University was one. It occurred to us that a series of short books discussing the 'Key Concepts' in political science would serve two purposes. In universities these books could provide the kind of brief political texts which might be of assistance to students in gaining a fuller understanding of the terms which they were constantly using. But we also hoped that outside the universities there exists a reading public which has the time, the curiosity and the inclination to pause to reflect on some of those words and ideas which are so often taken for granted. Perhaps even 'that insidious and crafty animal', as Adam Smith described the politican and statesman, will occasionally derive some pleasure or even profit from that more leisurely analysis which academic study can afford, and which a busy life in the practice of politics often denies.

It has been very far from the minds of those who have been concerned in planning and bringing into being the 'Key Concepts' series to try and impose (as if that were possible!) any uniform pattern on the authors who have contributed, or will contribute, to it. I, for one, hope that each author will, in his own individual manner, seek and find the best way of helping us to a fuller understanding of the concept which he has chosen to analyse. But whatever form the individual exposition may take, there are, I believe, three aspects of illumination which we can confidently expect from each volume in this series. First, we can look for some examination of the history of the concept, and of its evolution against a changing social and political background. I believe, as many do who are concerned with the study of political science, that it is primarily in history that the explanation must be sought for many of the perplexing problems of political analysis and judgement which beset us today. Second, there is the semantic aspect. To look in depth at a 'key concept' necessarily entails a study of the name which attached itself to it; of the different ways in which, and the different purposes for which, the name was used; of the way in which in the course of history the same name was applied to several concepts, or several names were applied to one and the same concept; and, indeed, of the changes which the same concept, or what appears to be the same concept, has undergone in the course of time. This analysis will usually require a searching examination of the relevant literature in order to assess the present stage of scholarship in each particular field. And thirdly, I hope that the reader of each volume in this series will be able to decide for himself what the proper and valid use should be of a familiar term in politics, and will gain, as it were, from each volume a sharper and better-tempered tool of political analysis.

There are many today who would disagree with Bismarck's view that politics can never be an exact science. I express no opinion on this much debated question. But all of us who are students of politics—and our numbers both inside and outside the universities continue to grow—will be the better for knowing what precisely we mean when we use a common political term.

London School of Economics and Political Science

Leonard Schapiro
General Editor

Acknowledgement

The publishers wish to thank George Allen & Unwin Ltd for permission to quote from Ernst Troeltsch, *The Social Teachings of the Christian Churches*.

1/Concepts of Social Movement

The English word 'movement' derives from the old French verb *movoir*, which means to move, stir or impel, and the medieval Latin *movimentum*. The general English usage of 'movement' to designate 'a series of actions and endeavours of a body of persons for a special object' (*Oxford Dictionary*) dates from the late eighteenth and early nineteenth centuries. This is still the most widely accepted usage of the term as applied to social phenomena.

A different and now obsolete usage of the term was to denote certain 'liberal', 'innovatory' or 'progressive' parties or functions as in *parti du mouvement* (French) or 'movement party' in early nineteenth-century Britain. For example, an anonymous commentator on the parliamentary scene at Westminster, writing in 1836, noted that 'Sir Robert Peel may at all times rely on the vociferous applause of the Tories, Lord John Russell on that of the Whigs, and Mr. O'Connell on that of the Radical or Movement party'.[1]

A third, and far from obsolete, usage of the term refers to 'historical tendency', 'trend', 'current' or 'drift'. Historians have a fondness for 'discovering' a historical movement of this kind, or using 'movement' as a *deus ex machina* to resolve their problems of explanation and interpretation. It is usually convenient if these historical forces or tendencies are implied to be beyond rational human control or direction. While such usages raise interesting questions about the role of the unconscious in historical interpretation, they confront those historians and philosophers who deploy them with colossal theoretical problems as soon as they try to define their concepts of historical movement with any theoretical precision. Marx, who employed several different usages of the term 'movement', encountered severe difficulties in his discussion of *historical movements*, for he was attempting an ambitious theory of a specific kind of movement, namely the proletarian social movement, by means of his theory of general historical movements.

In terms of general usage, both in England and in other European countries, the first usage listed above, i.e. a social movement as *a series of actions and endeavours of a body of persons for a special object*, has been generally predominant since the early nineteenth century. One of the earliest English examples is afforded by the successful pamphleteer and publicist William Cobbett who commented in connection with disorders among the poor in 1812: 'This is the circumstance that will most puzzle the ministry. They can find no agitators. It is a movement of the people's own.'[2]

If we follow the suggestive lead given by Raymond Williams in his *Culture and Society 1750–1950* (1958), 'movement' can be seen to be one of a family of certain key words (such as 'industry', 'democracy', 'class' and 'culture') in which a 'general pattern of change can be seen, and it can be used as a special kind of map by which it is possible to look again at those wider changes in life and thought to which changes in language evidently refer'. Like so many closely related words and ideas—'ideology', 'collectivism', 'communism', 'masses', 'proletariat' and 'solidarity'—the word 'movement' and its structure of meanings itself reflects cultural movements, changes in thought and feeling of some significance.

Among the historians and men of letters of the early nineteenth century, the term 'movement' was appealing because of its connotations with the newly fashionable and increasingly influential physical and mechanical sciences. With its overtones of dynamics, forces and powers, 'movement' offered to historians and social thinkers and critics an analogy of extraordinary attractiveness. Raymond Williams usefully reminds us of Carlyle's words:

> Not the external and physical alone is now managed by machinery, but the internal and spiritual also . . . Men are grown mechanical in head and in heart, as well as in hand. They have lost faith in individual endeavour, and in natural force, of any kind. Not for internal perfection, but for external combinations and arrangements, for institutions and constitutions, for Mechanism of one sort or another do they hope and struggle.[3]

The early usage and conceptualization of social movement can in part be seen as a 'mechanistic' response to the need for historical and social explanations of the contemporary world. As will be shown, this response was fraught with dangerous interpretative traps and confusions, but this only became clear as later attempts were made to clarify and refine the concept of social movement, and to develop theories of movements.

Second, and very important, 'movement' became a laudatory word for certain kinds of group activity which accorded well with the growing acceptance of the ideas of political democracy. It was an infinitely better term than the pejorative term 'mob'. And here it is difficult to agree with Williams that the term 'masses' replaced 'mob'. 'Masses' did partially replace the term mob for a small band of social critics and commentators perhaps, but it was among the general population and particularly among the working-class participants and leaders of political groups that the term 'movement' was rapidly and eagerly appropriated. It had never been a term of contempt such as 'mob' and later 'masses' were to become. To the English middle classes of the nineteenth century the mob was a wild thing, a monstrous beast to be contained at all costs lest it devour the property and persons of the worthy and respectable. The middle classes would have echoed Mr Pickwick's very sound piece of advice on self preservation to Mr Snodgrass:

> Pickwick: 'It is always best on these occasions to do what the mob do.'
>
> 'But suppose there are two mobs?' suggested Mr. Snodgrass.
>
> 'Shout with the largest,' replied Mr. Pickwick.[4]

The term mob implied, notes Williams, '. . . gullibility, fickleness, herd-prejudice, lowness of taste and habit. The masses, on this evidence, formed the perpetual threat to culture.'[5]

The term 'movement', on the other hand, implied autonomy, self-generated and independent action, control and leadership, a mechanism of organization and disciplined following in place of an untamed surging crowd. It carried the ring of dignity, status and self-confidence.

The word 'movement', like the words 'people', 'popular', 'democracy', 'equality' and 'liberty', is still universally regarded as what T. D. Weldon calls a 'hurrah! word'.[6] Every group, every political, religious or cultural minority aspires to become a 'movement'. Parties and groups of every ideological persuasion claim proudly to be part of a national or international 'movement', claim to have the support of their own youth movements, women's movements, labour movements, peasant movements. In recent years among student protesters, peace campaigners, anti-Vietnam War groups and civil rights crusades, the rhetoric of 'movement' has maintained its irresistible and universal appeal. Even such staid organizations as the British Labour party and the TUC, as if aware of their need to sustain *élan*, a combative spirit, and, above all, solidarity, attempt to keep the rhetoric of movement alive. 'Movement' still pumps some adrenalin into their congresses and assemblies.

The rhetoric of movement may almost be said to have its own momentum. Indeed, the more any protest group, organization or campaign appears to be under pressure, or in danger of collapse, the more it hankers for the reassurance of the rhetoric. Leaders of tiny fringe groups like to speak as if thousands of supporters, or potential followers await the command to advance. They talk as if decisive victory were within their grasp. They are, of course, simply whistling in the dark, and what they are afraid of is that if they were to stop whistling nothing more would be heard of them.

The reassuring resonance of movement rhetoric may partly explain the abiding popularity of its usage among movement activists. It should be noted, however, that the *literati* have found the language of movement equally, if not more, appealing. A leading political scientist, W. J. M. Mackenzie, shrewdly observed in 1967 that the study of movements has attracted intellectuals to a far greater extent than the study of, for example, international bureaucracies. He is surely correct in suggesting, as a reason for this, that movements are inherently intellectually romantic. Indeed, I think one can say that most who have chosen to write about social 'movements' have found this often ill-defined concept rich in allusion and connotation.

There is the fact that the movement concept is very closely linked to the concept of culture. The language, ideas and styles of movements inevitably reflect wider cultural changes and can often be found to be important in themselves as agencies of cultural change. Social movement has, therefore, important expressive and aesthetic dimensions revealing both cultural distinctiveness and assimilatory tendencies in the wider society. Recent interpretative work, and the work of the sociologists of symbolic interaction in America, have emphasized the importance of these symbolic and expressive facets of social movement. Some have gone so far as to relate them to theories of 'sociodrama', the 'theatre of revolution' and rituals of confrontation.

Then there is a suggestive cluster of connotations with physical movement. This does not simply apply to the 'massing', 'stirring' and 'turbulence' of social movement, but more generally to geographic movement of sects, refugees, exiles, migrants, colonists, missionaries, crusaders and seekers after promised lands.[7] Eric Hoffer, in 1951, and others have pointed out how, very often, the strength and unity of a mass movement may be enhanced by such migrations. Often a counter-movement in response to the mass movement's settlement, crusade or conquest, is implied.

Finally, the appeal of three obvious but extremely important strengths or advantages of the term 'movement' for historians and social theorists must be stressed. Firstly, the term is culturally interchangeable; secondly, it is ideologically neutral; and thirdly, 'movements' like 'ideologies' can be projected backward or forward in time.

Despite these advantages, and the popular and widespread usages of the term 'movement', the recent efforts to define and operationalize a concept of social movement have been beset by extraordinary confusion and difficulty. It is now necessary to consider some of these difficulties. We must also ask whether the tasks of conceptualizing and theorizing about social movement constitute a worthwhile or potentially valuable activity.

Concepts

It is possible to analyse the difficulties encountered in refining the social movement concept under five main headings: the problem of generality, dangers of ambiguity, problems of reification, problems of the 'type' concept, and problems of comparison.

Common usage may be a very unsound guide in the formulation of concepts for the social sciences, but its influence is hard to ignore. The problem is that the term 'movement' has become all things to all men. Mackenzie, for example, writing from a political scientist's point of view, argues that although political science cannot afford to neglect politicized movements, it is very difficult, in practice, to prevent such work from becoming 'all-inclusive and therefore vacuous'. (Mackenzie, 1967.) Many writers have used the term almost interchangeably with such words as 'organization', 'association', 'group' and 'union'. They sometimes appear to have hit on the word quite arbitrarily or for purely stylistic reasons.

This poses the question: What precisely distinguishes a social movement from other forms of group activity such as unions, pressure groups and parties? What, essentially, constitutes a social movement?

The most serious ambiguity is the blurring of the distinction between the historians' use of the concept of a general historical trend or movement, and a self-proclaimed social movement. In practice it is very difficult to maintain a clear distinction. Nevertheless the wilful conflation of the two usages gives rise to much pseudo-history. A very frank reviewer recently complained, 'How historians . . . love this word "movement"! And how unaware of their participation in such a conveniently well-organized, well-defined team are most of those contemporaries, thus mobilized at the time. Historians should beware of the word . . .'[8] It is essential that the distinction between movement as *deus ex machina*, and the self-professed 'social' movement should be clearly drawn, and that the historian or social scientist should know what kind of movement he is talking about.

A very real problem with all historical and sociological concepts is the constant tendency to reify them. Such reifications are necessarily reductionist: they concentrate on specific movement characteristics or aspects at the expense of others and this entails an inevitable degree of distortion when the concepts are related to empirical realities. A sociologist of religion, Bryan Wilson, makes the point very strongly:

> The types that sociologists construct are reifications. Their inherent danger is that, instead of being useful short-hand summaries of crucial elements in the empirical cases they claim to epitomise, they become caricatures remote from empirical phenomena . . . They may then be manipulated on a stage projected by the sociological imagination: the supposed model of the outworking of social processes would thus become a puppet show operated by principles not to be discovered in the real world, but with all the seductive attractiveness of comprehensibility and inherent natural order.[9]

An unwitting distortion of social processes in the real world frequently results from the reification of one specific variety of movement in a particular temporal or cultural context. This is then generalized into the archetypal social movement. This difficulty arises, for example, in Hannah Arendt's erudite and valuable work, *The Burden of Our Time* (1951). Though the author begins by making it clear that she is concentrating on the origins and character of totalitarian movements she repeatedly blurs the real distinction between totalitarian political movements and the diversity of movements in general. She emphasizes the 'absoluteness of movements which more than anything else separates them from party structures', and claims that the very name 'movement' alluded to the 'profound distrust for all parties'[10] shared by many at the turn of the century. These generalizations may hold in the case of certain totalitarian movements, but the reader must constantly be asking himself, 'To which specific movements do these characterizations apply?' It will be suggested in later discussion of the problems of evaluation and interpretation that the confusion is not merely confined to the reader, and that such reifications ultimately vitiate certain of the conclusions of Arendt's study.

Logically connected with the problems of reification are the pitfalls of type-concepts. Social movement is itself a type-concept, in that it must necessarily be related to a wider typology of social institutions, collectivities and phenomena; and it raises simultaneous problems of defining social movement types and sub-types. There is also a very real danger that, in the complex and relatively richly researched field of empirical studies of social movements, types will become as numerous as cases. A careful and vigilant utilization of typologies is essential in order to produce sociological generalization and to develop hypotheses.

At the same time, the articles in the volume edited by Wilson, *Patterns of Sectarianism*, and such detailed and penetrating studies as those of Hobsbawm (1959) and Cohn (1957) highlight the important divergences between movements, differences resulting from variations in cultural and historical contexts. Thus the contributions in Wilson's volume show the patent inadequacy of Ernst Troeltsch's early church/sect typification. (Troeltsch, 1931.) In the light of current knowledge it would be quite wrong to assume that all religious movements have basically similar ideologies, forms of organization, circumstances of origin, or patterns of development. The same holds true for nationalist movements, movements of the peasantry, movements of the industrial working class and for highly politicized movements of the twentieth century. In all these areas the concept of social movement is constantly being redefined and re-applied. Typologies can provide an invaluable conceptual tool, but only provided that they reflect concrete differences in the social processes and interrelationships of the social phenomena concerned. The validity and utility of type-concepts can only be judged in terms of the 'pay-off' they provide in suggesting possible fields and problems for research, and by their contribution to the methodology of empirical research and the development of social theory.

Let us suppose that it is possible, with constant vigilance, to avoid the worst pitfalls of reification and the problems of constructing typologies. If our type-concepts have been carefully thought out and related to studies of empirical phenomena, then their most valuable, if not their primary, function will be to assist in the tasks of comparison. From the questions: 'Is *x* a movement?' and, 'If so, what *kind* of movement?', it is essential to proceed to the problems: 'How does *x* compare with other movements of the same type or sub-type?' and, 'Has *x* any characteristics or patterns of origin or development in common with movements of other types?' and so forth.

A very real danger in the task of comparison lies in the fact that to isolate certain common aspects or dimensions of social movement as subjects for selective comparison would appear to be more manageable than a full-scale inter-movement comparison 'in the round'. The major disadvantages of this procedure are: 1. movements entirely lacking the chosen dimension (or in which it is not a marked characteristic) will be discounted in the comparison; 2. the selected dimensions for comparison may provide a purely arithmetical or configurative comparison which has no heuristic or explanatory relevance; and 3. (a rather more serious objection) the comparison thus produced may be used as the basis of a rank-order or hierarchy of social movements to import, by the back-door, a theory of the relative importance of certain movements. Such procedures are, of course, entirely subjective, or else based on arbitrary or inadequate premises.

Some comparative approaches of this kind are based on the assumption that the most 'significant' social movements are those with the most systematic and comprehensive ideologies. Others discount movements which do not succeed in developing any durable and firm organizational structure, or those which are short-lived. The internationally renowned British historian of the Bolshevik Revolution and its aftermath, E. H. Carr, has admitted to holding what is possibly the crudest of all these criteria of significance, that is the criterion of numbers, the sheer size of a movement's following or membership. Having quoted, with approbation, Lenin's dictum, 'Politics begin where the masses are; not where there are thousands, but where there are millions, that is where serious politics begin', Carr goes on to assert:

> These nameless millions were individuals acting more or or less unconsciously, together, constituting a social force. The historian will not in ordinary circumstances need to take cognizance of a single discontented peasant or discontented village. But millions of discontented peasants in thousands of villages are a factor no historian will ignore... Nor need we be perturbed by the platitude that movements are started by minorities. All effective movements have few leaders and a multitude of followers; but this does not mean that the multitude is not essential to their success. Numbers count in history.[11]

In fairness to Professor Carr it is true that many others have plumped for the same criterion of 'significance'. The assumption that 'numbers count' is in harmony with recent fashions in quantification in the social sciences and humanities. Some find it reassuring to have something concrete to measure and upon which to found explanations. However, the belief that 'you cannot argue with numbers' has never convinced the leaders or followers of movements. Some of the most interesting movements started as small minorities and remained small minorities. Their 'significance' does not lie in the successful mustering of large battalions, but as carriers of ideas, as harbingers of cultural and intellectual developments. The Oxford Movement or the Life and Liberty Movement in the Church of England may never have achieved 'mass following' or organization, yet it would be a rash historian of the Church of England who ignored their influence. Similarly, in the realm of intellectual movements, it would be impossible to write an intelligent account of twentieth-century European art without reference to surrealist or futurist movements whose active participants could probably have been numbered only in hundreds. Such 'league-table' approaches to the comparative study of social movements, whatever their basis, are, I would suggest, entirely unhelpful.

This must suffice as an exploratory review of some fundamental problems involved in defining and articulating the concept of social movement. Even a superficial reading of the literature makes it clear that there is no consensus even within disciplines as to how these difficulties may be overcome. Sociologists, social anthropologists and political scientists have of necessity improvised their own attempt at conceptual definition, often disagreeing among themselves. Some of these attempts will now be surveyed. Partially utilizing these efforts, we shall then attempt to construct a general working concept of social movement which would be generally applicable to all the social sciences and to history.

The pioneer attempt to define a 'scientific' concept of social movements and to deploy the concept in an ambitious social theory was made by the German, Lorenz von Stein, in his *The History of the Social Movement in France, 1789–1850*, first published in 1850. Instead of surveying the French Revolution and its aftermath from the point of view of changes in governmental structure or personnel, Stein stressed its significance as a series of endeavours to create a new society. Stein attempted, as Dr Mengelberg has justifiably claimed, 'to set up a concept of society as an independent term and to develop its content'.[12] Moreover, Stein conceived of the structure of society as fundamentally determining political change.

In common with Marx, Stein rejected the idealism of Hegel's universal state in which the state and society were conceived as coterminous. He was convinced of the social realities of social conflict and its resultant alienations and antagonisms: 'Since life represents a constant struggle of the personal self-determining element with the non-personal and natural elements, the life of the human community is a permanent struggle between the state and society . . .'[13]

Stein also shared Marx's historical materialism in his emphasis on the importance of material self-interest of individuals and classes, as an engine of social change. 'Interest,' wrote Stein, 'which is the centre of all human interaction and therefore *of all social motion*, is the principle of society.'[14]

From these premises Stein deduced that class interests and class conflicts were of decisive importance. He developed the concept of the proletariat, quite independently of Marx and Engels, and applied it to the rising industrial working classes massing in cities of Western Europe. Stein regarded the proletariat's turbulence, discontents, and efforts at mass action as the crucial development of his age. He therefore reified the working-class efforts towards organization and economic and political power as 'the social movement'. Stein's special use of the concept of social movement remained influential among the school of German and Austrian historians of socialism throughout the nineteenth century. Like Stein, they regarded the movements of the working class as constituting 'the social movement', and, following Stein, they became preoccupied with developing prescriptive theories of methods of peacefully assimilating the proletariat into the wider society.

Werner Sombart was one of the better known later representatives of this school. In his *Socialism and the Social Movement* (1896), Sombart defines the movement as 'the conception of all the attempts at emancipation on the part of the proletariat'.[15] On occasion Sombart's polemics got the better of him and he became quite lyrical: 'Never in all history have so many individuals combined to form a united movement; never in all history was the solid phalanx of the masses so plainly the characteristic of a movement as in that of the proletariat . . . To picture the Social Movement of our day . . . we must imagine a huge wave of humanity, from which scarcely one individual stands out, covering the dry land to the distant horizon.'[16]

Ferdinand Tönnies in his renowned *Gemeinschaft und Gesellschaft* (1887), a book which was little known until the turn of this century, developed his concept of the 'social collective'. This concept, though it does not use the term 'movement' has, in fact, considerable relevance to the development of the social movement concept.

First, Tönnies clearly distinguishes between a 'social organization' and a 'social collective'. A 'social organization' is a corporate body which is pure artefact and which 'is never anything natural, neither can it be understood as a mere physical phenomenon',[17] whereas the 'social collectives . . . rest partly on natural and partly on physical collectives'.[18] Tönnies held that their essence was to be found in their basis of natural and psychological relationships and the fact that they are consciously affirmed and willed. These emphases upon the socio-psychological character of the collective and upon the importance of conscious volition anticipate much contemporary discussion. Tönnies, however, felt unable to free his concept of social collective from that of class and estate: 'This phenomenon [of social collective] . . . is especially in evidence in the distinguishing characteristic through which certain classes are given prominence, nobility and authority.'[19]

Tönnies conceives his social collective, then, as 'partly an objective phenomenon and partly something positive in the people's consciousness'.[20] These ideas are very suggestive, but the ensuing discussion becomes preoccupied with the problem of the consciousness of class struggle which Tönnies interpreted as becoming more acute and general than the earlier conflicts between estates.

A far more recent attempt at a thorough-going definition of the concept of social movement was made by Rudolf Heberle in his *Social Movements: An Introduction to Political Sociology* (1951). Heberle set himself the ambitious task of 'the development of a comparative, systematic theory of social movements within a more comprehensive system of sociology'.[21]

Heberle accepts one traditional emphasis of the German students of social movements, that is that the main distinguishing feature of a social movement is that it aims to introduce radical changes in the social order, especially in the fields of property distribution and labour relations. He rejects Stein's exclusive identification of the concept with proletarian movements in industrial societies. Clearly, for Heberle, the concept has a far wider applicability—for example, to peasant, nativistic and Fascist movements. Heberle also assimilates Tönnies' emphasis on conscious volition which was developed in relation to his concept of the 'social collective'. He conceives of social movements as 'a special kind of social group of a particular structure. Although containing among their members certain groups that are formally organized, the movements *as such* are not organized groups'.[22] Again he is here following Tönnies (and acknowledges his debt) by drawing a distinction between a social movement and a corporate group. The conceptual requirement of group consciousness, a sense of group identity and solidarity, necessarily involves Heberle in excluding unconscious 'trends or tendencies' from the social movement concept.

Heberle distinguishes two other criteria. First, social movements are always integrated by a specific pattern of normative commitments, 'constitutive ideas', or ideology. Second, social movements are not necessarily nationally confined; they may be multinational, international or supra-national in character. He holds that all social movements fulfil two key functions in societies: they help both in the formation of the common will or political group will, and in the process of socialization, training and recruitment of political élites.

Clearly Heberle can be seen to have travelled a considerable distance towards freeing the concept of social movement from the constricting formulations of Stein and Sombart. Heberle's very real progress in clarification does not, however, succeed in resolving some serious conceptual difficulties.

First, Heberle retains the quasi-Marxist preoccupation with links and interactions between social classes and social movements: 'The particular significance of an appeal to a certain social class or classes is now generally recognized . . . Social movements . . . are therefore as a rule closely bound to certain social classes and opposed by others.' The passage concludes by asserting baldly that 'the political and social ideas of an epoch or a society are an expression of the class structure and the state of economic development of that society'.[23] Thus Heberle is reifying from specific historical forms of social movements, and implying a somewhat dogmatic theory of social movement and social class.

Second, there is a more serious set of conceptual difficulties posed by Heberle's attempt to distinguish between 'genuine social movements'[24] or 'movements of profound historical significance' and minor, smaller, more ephemeral movements or protest movements.[25] It does seem that Heberle's approach is unnecessarily arbitrary in that it excludes, on these grounds, such phenomena as student movements and strike movements.

In a recent article (1968) Heberle has reiterated the view that all major social movements have the distinguishing characteristic of 'a more or less elaborate' ideology or 'set of constitutive ideas' which have the aim of remaking the socio-economic and political orders, and upon which action programmes are based.

This claim is augmented by the sweeping historical hypothesis that revolutionary movements of this kind are the unique concomitant of the process of secularization. Heberle argues that such movements are uniquely identified with the development of secular ideologies, that is with a *specific* aspect of the development of Western thought since the eighteenth century. Now whether or not this hypothesis stands up to close historical investigation is irrelevant to our present argument (though it is a widely held theory which will be discussed more extensively in connection with theories of the origin of movements). The important point is surely that there is no prima facie reason why we should accept this specific type of social movement in a particular cultural and historical context as inherently more 'historically significant' or 'genuine' than any other.

Two other recent efforts at conceptualization have deployed

social movement as a type-concept within a general theory of collective behaviour. Herbert Blumer in 1957 proposed a two-headed conceptualization assimilating the historian's concept of unconscious tendency or trend: 'Whatever be its type, a social movement signifies either a collective effort to transform some given area of established social relations, or else a large unguided change involving, however unwittingly, large numbers of participants.'[26]

As examples of unorganized changes Blumer cites the extension of democratic philosophy, and the growth of interest in science. Blumer's double-barrelled conceptualization, however, has not been adopted by those working in the area of empirical movement studies.

An ambitious theory of collective behaviour incorporating social movement as a type-concept was formulated by Neil Smelser in 1962 in his *Theory of Collective Behavior*. Smelser makes a sharp division between 'norm-oriented movements' (for example, social reform movements) and 'value-oriented movements' (for example, religious and revolutionary movements). He makes a further distinction between norm- and value-oriented movements and 'panic responses', 'craze responses' and 'hostile outbursts'.

Smelser proceeds to construct a theory of the determinants of collective behaviour, including social movements, by utilizing the 'logic of value-added', employed by Samuelson and others in economics, and a Parsonian theory of social action.

Smelser admits that 'many . . . necessary conditions must be present for any kind of collective episode to occur', but argues that these determinants must combine in a particular pattern. He asserts that 'as they combine, the determination of the type of episode . . . becomes increasingly specific, and alternative behaviors are ruled out as possibilities'.[27] It will be necessary to consider Smelser's theory in some detail as it applies to the origins and characterization of movement. However, certain of what he calls 'major determinants' of an episode mark out Smelser's implicit conceptualization of social movement. He envisages such movements arising in the context of severe strain, for example, economic depression or defeat in war, in the wider society; that a prerequisite for their development is the growth and spread of a generalized norm-oriented or value-oriented belief; and that participants must be mobilized for action in the form of movement activity.

The positivist determinism of Smelser's theory demands critical examination. Moreover, there is a very real conceptual problem involved in his rigid separation of norm- and value-oriented movement. The norm/value distinction is helpful only if it is both precisely defined and meaningful in its application to real movements. In practice one movement's norm may be another movement's value. It depends where you are standing at the time. In the deep American South the existence of discrimination against Negroes has for long been a norm. To the Negroes seeking the abolition of such discrimination the achievement of civil rights and social equality has become a value. If men regard themselves as the victims of oppression and injustice under the existing laws and practices of society, then the removal of such oppression becomes an absolutely valued end regardless of the particular method they may adopt to achieve it.

It may be possible to find examples of solely norm-oriented movement. However, social movements are rarely one-dimensional; they tend to be multi-dimensional. That is to say they may be concerned simultaneously with values, norms, forms of organization and material conditions and resources. The Nazi and Bolshevik movements, for example, were characterized by absolutist ideologies: both claimed to be ushering in the 'new world'. Yet in the very act of mobilizing and organizing their movements in opposition, and in their climbs to power, these movements imposed their own normative commitments, codes of conduct, rules of 'democratic centralism', codes of deference to the leadership, and so forth. Any conceptualization of movements which attempts to ignore this rich diversity among movements and their often self-contradictory features will become lost in the foggy unreality of its own abstractions. Smelser's difficulties in large part arise from his rigid acceptance of Parsons' hierarchy of 'components of social action':

1 values
2 norms
3 mobilization into organized roles
4 situational facilities

In defining his concept of value-oriented movement, for example, he is driven to assert that any collective attempt to 'restore, protect, modify or create values in the name of a generalized belief . . . necessarily involves all the components of action

. . .'[28] Such an all-embracing definition clearly cannot accommodate a wide range of cultural, intellectual and 'moral protest' movements. Many such movements such as Emmanuel Mounier's Personalist Movement, the British Humanist Movement or the Vietnam War Moratorium see their basic function as the expression of dissent over values. They regard the expression and publicizing of their dissent as a worthwhile end in itself. Though they are, in Smelser's terms, 'value-oriented' they are inherently unprepared and unequipped to attempt both the redefinition of norms and a reorganization of the motivations of individuals in addition to redefining situational facilities. Smelser's norm-oriented/value-oriented typification lacks a convincing rationale and could be usefully discarded.

A working concept?

Now we must turn to the second question raised at the beginning of our review of concepts. Is it possible to salvage from the diversity and confusion of conceptualizations of social movement, a general working concept which is of inter-disciplinary applicability? Such a concept would need to achieve a fine balance between comprehensiveness, flexibility and the empirical requirements of scholars. The proposed working concept, therefore, requires a certain generality of definition. It is entirely inappropriate for one particular discipline, such as social history or sociology, to attempt to appropriate and monopolize the use of a concept which can only be adequately deployed and related to empirical phenomena by the combined, and often collaborative, efforts of historians, sociologists, social anthropologists, political scientists and psychologists.

Admittedly this is an extremely demanding specification, and the reader confronted with the complete absence of consensus in the literature could be forgiven if he was tempted to throw in the towel. The present contribution to the discussion is, however, undertaken in the conviction that it is both possible and desirable to define a general working concept of social movement which is potentially of heuristic value.

It is proposed that our working concept should attempt to identify and generally define the quintessential characteristics of social movement. The presence of all these characteristics may thus be defined as a precondition of social movement.

1 *A social movement is a deliberate collective endeavour to promote change in any direction and by any means, not excluding violence, illegality, revolution or withdrawal into 'utopian' community*. Social movements are thus clearly different from *historical* movements, tendencies or trends. It is important to note, however, that such tendencies and trends, and the influence of the unconscious or irrational factors in human behaviour, may be of crucial importance in illuminating the problems of interpreting and explaining social movement.

2 *A social movement must evince a minimal degree of organization, though this may range from a loose, informal or partial level of organization to the highly institutionalized and bureaucratized movement and the corporate group*. Indeed, it will be shown that much of the literature of social movements has been concerned with natural histories, models or theories of movement development. Such models have attempted to simulate changes in movement structure and organization ranging from stages of initial social unrest and excitement and the emergence of a charismatic leadership, to a revolutionary movement's seizure of power.

3 *A social movement's commitment to change and the* raison d'être *of its organization are founded upon the conscious volition, normative commitment to the movement's aims or beliefs, and active participation on the part of the followers or members*. This particular characterization of social movement in terms of volition and normative commitment is endorsed by something approaching a consensus among leading scholars in this field. Heberle, for example, conceives of these belief-systems as an expression of the collective will of the people among whom they are accepted. He is emphatic that it is the element of volition that makes the beliefs socially effective. It is the conscious volition of individuals acting collectively that brings about the embodiment of ideologies in social movements. (Heberle, 1968)

The social anthropologist Anthony Wallace (writing in 1968) holds that participants in movements actually alter their behaviour and rationalize their new pattern of behaviour in terms of the movement's beliefs. A. Etzioni in his 1961 analyses of complex organizations stresses that certain organizations can only elicit the adherence of their members by means of promoting and instilling a normative commitment to the organization. It is true, however, that extraneous inducements may partly or wholly replace normative commitments for numerous individual members. They may join, or continue membership, because they are greedy for power, money or prestige. Nevertheless, it is widely agreed that no social movement, properly speaking, can be developed or sustained without a widespread diffusion of normative commitment to the movement's beliefs among the participants.

As Heberle and others have made clear, the element of normative commitment is by no means unitary. There is a considerable literature typologizing its major forms. Heberle, in an article written in 1968, makes use of Weber's typology and identifies three major types of commitment: the value-rational fellowship of believers; the emotional-affectual following of the charismatic leader; and the purposive-rational association for pursuing individual interests. In practice, these types very often combine or overlap within the same social movement.

It is worth spelling out what is implicit in this stress on normative commitment as a precondition of social movement. It implies that all social movements are to some degree spontaneous, self-directing and autonomous. For example, the real strength of successful popular guerrilla movements in Asia and elsewhere (as America has found to her cost) is their highly autochthonous character, the strength of popular commitment to their cause. (Hence the sad irony of John F. Kennedy's remark that the most vital battle to be fought, in such conditions, was the battle for minds.)

It may be objected that some organizations calling themselves movements have not been spontaneously created or autonomous at any stage in their development. The *Hitler Jugend* would be such a case. Such a 'movement', like the trade union 'movement' in Stalin's Russia, was the passive creature of the totalitarian movement. Created by *diktat*, and with compulsory membership, such organizations are mere appendages and creatures of the state bureaucracy. They find it necessary, however, for purposes of external propaganda, and internal indoctrination, to adopt the rhetoric of movement and to purport to express a normative commitment which can in reality never be freely given or openly withheld.

In dictatorships lacking the full range of totalitarian sanctions, such organizations (for example the Spanish government-run Union of Students) are treated with scathing contempt by the general population. Such organizations can be termed *ersatz* movements to distinguish them from social movements. They stand in utter contrast to such spontaneous and self-directing youth movements as the pre-Nazi German *wandervogel* or the now world-wide scout movement.[29] Social movements are not interchangeable with government-controlled agencies, though they may on occasion offer to support a government, or government agency, of their own free will. On the contrary, they may on occasion, as Mackenzie puts it, 'claim a legitimacy higher than the state',[30] and they may develop the capacity to carry their ideas across frontiers.

The general working concept of social movement outlined here is closely related to, and to some extent overlaps with, other type-concepts of group activity such as 'political party', 'pressure group', 'trade union' and 'voluntary association'.

Basically defined, a political party is an alliance or coalition for the purposes of competing for political office and power. Our definition follows Schumpeter's, made in 1942, and brings out the fact that political parties do not necessarily have common ideologies or belief-systems. Neither is it necessary that they have a popular or mass following. The old parties of parliamentary caucus and faction in eighteenth-century England could not correctly be termed social movements. Nevertheless, it is true that most modern political parties have a movement dimension. As Jean Blondel argues, they increasingly tend to be mass parties with well-defined policies and programmes. Some political parties contain more than one movement: for example, the US Democratic party has contained simultaneously large sections of the labour movement, and various ethnic movements. Some movements use political parties as the spearhead of their action in seeking political power, but also engage in action at pressure group, educational or cultural levels. This obviously applies to the Communist movements of Western European countries. For some movements, however, political party activity is considered either irrelevant to their purposes or entirely profitless. For this reason, millenarian movements and anarchist movements, for example, rarely foster any connection with political parties. The important point to note is that many protest movements, religious movements, moral crusades, and intellectual and cultural movements are *sui generis*.

The social movement is their unique and most appropriate form. Therefore, though the student of social movements rapidly becomes aware of the frequent overlap and close connection between highly politicized social movements and political parties, especially in highly industrialized societies, this relation cannot be generalized to social movements of all types in all cultural contexts.

Similarly, many movements engage in pressure group activity and may indeed develop into formally organized purpose-rational associations engaged solely in pressure-group action. An example of this would be the major part of the American labour movement. American unions long ago lost their normative commitment to any belief in socialism as a trade-union ideology. Indeed in the USA most unions never firmly adopted any such creed. Unions have traditionally eschewed direct involvement as political parties and restrict their activities to pressure group lobbying within the major parties, and directly with government departments and agencies and private employers.

Clearly, however, accommodation to the role of pressure group considerably restricts the movement's range of action. Acceptance of the norms and procedures of pressure group activity implies acceptance of the legitimacy of the government, the constitution, the legal norms governing bargaining and the enforcement of contracts, etc. Now it is well known that many movements do not accept these conditions of pressure group action. Movements diametrically opposed to the political system in power, such as revolutionary and resistance movements or the movements of the disfranchised or the oppressed, feel cast out, excluded or alienated from the political system and therefore from the bargaining system. Rather than do business with the 'devil' such movements can refuse to pay taxes, can riot in the streets or be driven by their bitter antipathy to the regime to a shooting rebellion, an assassination, sabotage or guerrilla resistance.

Critics may object that our working concept of social movement is so broad that it is interchangeable with the term 'voluntary association'. Many voluntary associations such as the Howard League for Penal Reform or the United Nations Association are indeed social movements in the terms of our concept for they involve a commitment to change, a measure of organization, and they depend upon the normative commitment and participation of their members. However, many voluntary associations do not involve a commitment to change, nor do they call for a necessary minimal degree of normative commitment to change or participation on the part of members. They may have purely mundane and utilitarian functions such as social mixing, entertainment and recreation: for example, drinking or gambling clubs, dancing groups and dining clubs. Many are simply commercial associations for insurance, saving or investment, such as the British United Provident Association and the friendly societies or building societies. They demand no normative commitment to change on the part of members. Nor do they seek or welcome participation by their rank and file. Day to day management is left entirely to a managing board or committee. Many voluntary associations, therefore, are not social movements in any sense. Some, however, have movement dimension in that at a particular period or among certain members they do demand a normative commitment to change and more active participation by rank-and-file members. In the early days of motoring the Automobile Association had this 'movement' character, at least among its hard core of pioneers and motoring devotees. It is doubtful if more than a handful of members now regard the AA as a movement, and most would be astonished if it were to rediscover its movement dimension and role.

It is also important to note the limitations of the 'voluntary association' concept itself. It covers a far narrower range of groups than the social movement concept we have sketched here. Though many secular social movements of Western Europe and North America have developed into purpose-rational associations and corporate groups, such movements are certainly not characteristic of non-Western societies. In many Asian and African societies, millenarian and religious movements, prophetic sects, cults and secret societies are more typical and profuse. Such movements evince a form of volition and normative commitment entirely alien to the purpose-rational voluntary association. Many are deeply interconnected with particularistic, ascriptive and kinship groups, and the basis of their pattern of beliefs or constitutive values derives from the emotional-affectual following of a prophet or charismatic leader. The social movement concept, therefore, is far more comprehensive in that it embraces these religious, millenarian and prophetic movements as well as those voluntary associations which have a movement dimension.

The distinction between social movement, political party, pressure group and voluntary association, is therefore a real one, despite many instances of overlap.

The major part of the ensuing discussion attempts to show the indispensable value of a working concept of social movement for social scientists and historians. Within the framework of a proposed typology of social movements, I hope to point out some of the major problems of explanation and interpretation that have been confronted by scholars in various areas of movement study. In addition, some of the seemingly inescapable normative, moral and political dilemmas, which leaders and followers of movements face, will be highlighted.

Before we embark on this review, however, it will be helpful to consider two extremely influential secular political ideologists of movement, Rousseau and Marx.

2/Rousseau, Marx and Movement

We shall make a convenient distinction throughout this study between ideologists, practitioners and scientists of social movement. Any individual whose major work and concern has been the formulation, elaboration and advocacy of normative or prescriptive theories or ideologies of society, may provide a source of ideological thinking and direction for a social movement, or for many social movements. In the case of a body of ideology that is particularly influential and widely disseminated, ideas derived from it will find their way into the general current of thought. Such major ideological sources will thus influence many participants unwittingly. Major ideologies may therefore be, to this extent, assimilated under *historical* movements, trends or tendencies. Nevertheless, in many cases, a minority social movement will consciously and consistently attempt to embody or realize the aims of an ideology quite unique to itself, and will expend much of its energies in ideological propaganda and public debate with its opponents.

The term 'practitioner' is self-explanatory. By 'scientist' of social movement we refer to those social scientists and historians who have attempted, with varying degrees of success, the objective description, interpretation and explanation of social movements.

These types are not, of course, mutually exclusive. Marx himself, for example, could claim to have worked at all three levels. So could many members of such influential schools as the *Philosophes*, and the Fabians. Men such as Owen, Babeuf and Bakunin maintained a fairly even balance between their contributions as original social thinkers and ideologists, and their work in initiating and leading movements. Even Adolf Hitler, the archetypal activist demagogue, made his own crude and warped attempt at an ideological *prise de position* in the pathological racism of *Mein Kampf*. In most cases, however, it is justifiable and useful to characterize an individual's predominant contributions to a social movement or movements as falling in one or other of the three categories.

In the case of Rousseau or Marx, for instance, the role of ideologist overshadows all else. On the other hand, Lenin, though he certainly made several distinctive contributions to the development of Marxist ideology, was *par excellence* a movement practitioner, organizer, conspirator and leader and can be accurately characterized as such. His conceptual framework, however, was overwhelmingly Marxist.[1] (We shall be considering his development of Marxist revolutionary theory, organization and tactics in chapter 7.)

It could be reasonably claimed that the two most influential secular ideologists of the past two hundred years are Rousseau and Marx: both have provided the richest source of constitutive values, concepts and beliefs for the whole range of contemporary socio-political movements. In so far as many critics have regarded the influence of both men on the ideologies of social movements as a baleful one, they have tended to blame Rousseau and Marx for what they regard as the damaging or destructive consequences of revolutionary history. It is, of course, unreasonable to hold that these thinkers are in some sense personally responsible for everything that has been done in their names or which has been justified by reference to vulgarized versions of their ideas. As Shlomo Avineri, in his discussion of Marx, has put it: 'A main target of historical research into Marxism may therefore be to rescue Marx from the hands of his disciples.'[2] Yet this admission does not imply that major ideologists are without any intellectual or moral responsibilities in terms of their own lives and works. This would be to dehumanize them, at best to reduce them to mere ghosts in the machine. Indeed both Rousseau and Marx were acutely aware of the explosive potential of 'revolutionaries of the pen'.

The particular means by which the ideologists' revolutionary thoughts were disseminated, and the historical circumstances at the time of their production, must not be overlooked. Their contemporary reading publics could not be fully aware of their complex and often self-contradictory intellectual development. Lacking the sympathetic insight and hindsight of modern critics and editors, contemporaries were unable to balance a 'young' Marx against the 'mature' Marx, or the Rousseau of the *Contrat Social* against the Rousseau of the *Discours sur l'Inégalité*. These authors came to their notice, if at all, not through the whole corpus of their works but through their essentially popular, readable, revolutionary popular texts. The *Contrat Social* (1762) achieved wide notice among the educated bourgeoisie of France, the very class to whom the anti-monarchical and popular revolutionary democracy of Rousseau would appeal. Likewise with Marx, the true 'Bible' of the working-class movement became not *Das Kapital* (1867) as Engels thought,[3] but *The Communist Manifesto* (1848), by Marx and Engels, which rapidly reached the industrial working classes throughout Europe and even penetrated backward Russia. These were books that inspired and re-directed movements, and, through these movements, changed the world. It was also not without significance that these publications coincided with periods of acute social discontent, turbulence and trouble: they sowed their seed in soil fertile for the revolutions their authors promised and desired.

In the manner characteristic of an ideology, Rousseau's account of the social pact and the ideal political association that is to be founded upon it begins by asserting several dogmatic propositions. The major part of the work is then devoted to filling out the implications of these propositions and to a polemic on the moral desirability of Rousseau's model body politic.

He begins by proclaiming his firm belief in the right of all men to organize in their collective interest, and their right to rebel against tyranny. He insists that, 'It must, then, be admitted that Might does not create Right, and that no man is under an obligation to obey any but the legitimate powers of the state.'[4]

The second fundamental proposition is that the only legitimate authority in human society is that founded upon the consent of the people: 'Since no man has natural authority over his fellows, and since Might can produce no Right, the only foundation left for legitimate authority in human societies is Agreement.'[5]

These twin assertions of the right of revolution and the legitimate supremacy of the popular will have been appropriated and reiterated by practically every secular, reformist or revolutionary ideology, and every Western politicized movement, in the past two hundred years. They have a superficial unassailability which has made them of universal appeal to demagogues, and especially to the disfranchised, outcast or oppressed. They seem to accord well with Rousseau's own rebellious, anarchic, anti-conventional characteristics shown more plainly in *Émile* and the *Discours sur l'Inégalité*.

Yet when one closely examines these assertions and the model political association Rousseau appears to envisage, one is compelled to agree with Professor J. L. Talmon (in his *The Origins of Totalitarian Democracy*, 1952), that the model is shot through with other tendencies powerfully in contradiction to Rousseau's writings on natural freedom: features of authoritarianism, collectivism, severe political discipline and even a rationalization of the use of political terror for the protection of the state. The paradox that liberal individualist democracy as well as collectivist *étatiste* democracy has asserted Rousseau's two initial propositions as fundamental principles is reflected in the contradiction of the *Contrat Social.* For the substitution of the absolute right of popular democracy for the 'divine right of kings' did not resolve the difficulty that the individual tyrant might be replaced by the tyranny of the majority or by a dictatorship of the minority acting in the name of the majority.

Rousseau's assumption was that popularly based tyranny would be avoided by the device of the 'general will'. The general will was seen as the highest expression of the purpose of the state, the embodiment of national solidarity and the nation's popular will. It was this mechanism which was to ensure complete harmony between the individual and the general will. 'Some form of association must be found,' argued Rousseau, 'as a result of which the whole strength of the community will be enlisted for the protection of the person and property of each constituent member in such a way that each, when united to his fellows, renders obedience to his own will, and remains as free as he was before.'[6] This anticipates, of course, Kant's categorical imperative, the elaboration of the idea that it may be necessary to force a man to be free.

For such an ideal association to work, Rousseau believes that it will be necessary for everyone to be given a sufficiency of wealth and that no individual should acquire more than his fair share. The state must ensure that this equality is achieved. All citizens are to be under the supreme direction of the general will. This general will 'is always right and ever tends to the public advantage'.[7] But the people will not always know the general will: 'It is ever the way of men to wish their own good, but they do not at all times see where that good lies.'[8] Rousseau goes on to distinguish between the will of all as the sum of individual wills, and the general will which is concerned only with the common interest. It follows that 'a legislator is necessary to guide the blind multitude' and to discover 'what is for its own good'.[9]

There are many more intimations of totalitarian democracy; for example, in the dogmatic assertion that 'whoever shall refuse to obey the general will must be constrained by the whole body of his fellow citizens to do so . . .'[10] There is the castigation of 'intriguing groups' and 'partial associations' and the injunction 'that there be no subsidiary groups within the State'.[11] Most unconsciously prophetic of all is the passage in which Rousseau justifies the liquidation of enemies of the people: '. . . the evil-doer who attacks the fabric of social right becomes, by reason of his crime, a rebel and a traitor to his country. By violating its laws he ceases to be a member of it, and may almost be said to have made war upon it . . . The preservation, therefore, of the State is seen to be incompatible with his own continued existence.'[12] We shall later observe that there is a series of firm connecting links between the absolutism of Rousseau's general will, the Jacobins, the Blanquists and Lenin's own revolutionary dictatorship. (Clarification of the French revolutionary stage in this tradition has been provided by Professor Talmon.)

At the same time, other aspects of Rousseau's concept of the general will, and his ideology of revolutionary democracy, require emphasis. The *Contrat Social* is not simply a blueprint for totalitarian democracy. Rousseau makes two highly significant contributions to the moulding of secular ideologies of revolution which are characteristic of most European social and political movements of the nineteenth century.

First there is, both implicit and explicit, Rousseau's *nationalism.* It is common to seek intellectual origins of revolutionary nationalism in the ideas of Kant, Fichte, Hegel and Renan; yet it is from Rousseau that nationalism as creed and doctrine derives its most vital and appealing ideological component. For Rousseau assumes throughout the *Contrat Social* that the inevitable and appropriate basis for the establishment of his ideal political association is the nation-state. The 'universal civilized society' and the general will as he conceives them are to be harmonized in the form of a republican nation-state. Moreover the nation he envisages will be immeasurably stronger than the old dynastic regimes. It will achieve absolute popular legitimacy and total solidarity. All internal enemies of the general will are to be eliminated for the protection of the state. Such a nation-state will clearly be in a position, according to Rousseau, to act with superior legitimacy and wisdom, and will be essentially morally superior to nations in the grip of arbitrary government or tyranny, or nations divided against themselves. The possibility that Rousseau does not explore in the *Contrat Social* is that the attempt by a republic to realize in practice the ideal body politic directed by the general will might bring it into conflict with other states. Strategies of international conflict and imperial expansion were to be elaborated by later ideologists of nationalism. Yet in the long term, Rousseau's emphases on legitimacy and solidarity constituted an invaluable recharging of the nation-state concept.

Second, there is an implicit and appealing revolutionism underlying the whole conception of *contrat social.* A simple theory of revolutionary development is implicit in the notion that the general will is, as it were, latent in the society of the old regime. The general will still remains to be identified and understood by the revolutionary leaders and followers (the rise of the revolutionary movement); it must then be enthroned (revolutionary seizure of power); and its opponents must be destroyed (elimination of counter-revolutionaries). Following the entrenchment of the revolutionary movement-regime Rousseau envisages the task of the legislator, the pilot of the revolution, as being the indoctrination of the people with correct revolutionary principles, the creation of a revolutionary kind of man, and the final ushering in of the new millennium. This imaginative and relatively early projection (1762) of the sequence of revolutionary development has more than prophetic significance. So widely did Rousseau's image of archetypal revolution permeate the ideologies of the late eighteenth century and the nineteenth and twentieth centuries, that it has almost the character of self-fulfilling prophecy. Perhaps understandably, his ideology of movement has occasionally been mistaken for the 'natural history' of revolution.

There is a rich variety of critical and interpretative works on Karl Marx's social and political thought, to which the reader is referred for analyses of Marx's philosophical contributions and development.[13] Marx's indebtedness to Hegelian thought and the influences of the 'Young Hegelians' are very widely documented. If there is a gap in this literature it lies in the absence of comprehensive scholarly accounts of other important intellectual precursors of Marxism. For example, Marx freely confessed his debt to the 'bourgeois historians and bourgeois economists' who developed the concept of classes and class struggle and first recognized their importance.[14] (The Scottish Philosophical Radicals were deploying the concept of class in the 1780s and '90s.) Such an account would also have to give due weight to the important influence of the Saint-Simonians and the historians of French Revolution, upon

Marx. There is no clear-cut evidence on the possibility of the specific influence of Lorenz von Stein's work on Marx, though it is highly probable that Marx was familiar with *The History of the Social Movement in France* (1850).

It is not our purpose to pursue these important questions of historical interpretation here. Nor is it relevant to our subject to attempt a detailed exposition of Marx's often subtle and elaborate theoretical refinements and modifications. Our purpose is rather to identify those key propositions of Marx which provided the ideological basis of many socialist and working-class movements. These propositions are dogmatically and boldly asserted in the polemical context of *The Communist Manifesto*. Their immediate impact was to astonish and excite by the daring of their synthesis and by the clarity and confidence of their historical prediction. The rest of Marx's career may be seen as a tremendous, almost Herculean, attempt to justify and vindicate these initial claims by means of a 'scientific' theory and by his active political commitment and constant injunctions to socialist movements.

Marx's basic propositions constitute a 'grand theory' of social and economic development, which is termed 'the historical movement'. The motor and regulator of social change, it is claimed, is the character of material production. The conditions of man's material existence determine his social relations; they determine his consciousness, and they create and regulate the development of classes and the pattern of class conflict. Thus the *Manifesto* argues: '. . . man's ideas, views and conceptions, in one word, man's consciousness, change with every change in the conditions of his material existence, in his social relations, and in his social life . . . What else does the history of ideas prove than that intellectual production changes its character in proportion as material production is changed? The ruling ideas of each age have been the ideas of its ruling class.'[15]

Whatever the 'history of ideas' might prove, Marx himself certainly provides no proof, but proceeds to a further bold dogma: 'The history of all past society has consisted in the development of class antagonisms, antagonisms that assumed different forms at different epochs. But whatever form they may have taken, one fact is common to all past ages, viz., the exploitation of one part of society by the other.'[16]

For Marx and Engels the key to understanding the forms of historical materialism and the processes of dichotomized class conflict is the theory of the 'dialectic' which is taken over from Hegelian philosophy. The historical movement does not proceed in an entirely incomprehensible and random manner, but rather by a series of organic evolutionary stages. Each stage is ushered in by a fresh revolution in the modes and social relations of production which can be causally explained as dialectic response to the changes in the real material conditions and class antagonisms of the society. This pattern of response-reaction-response takes the form of thesis, (movement), antithesis, (counter-movement), and synthesis, (the fusion or reconciliation of thesis and antithesis). Thus the rise of the bourgeoisie and the process of capital accumulation can be regarded as a 'thesis' to which the revolutionary movement of the proletariat was the 'antithesis', and the 'synthesis' is envisaged as the birth of the new classless Communist society.

The difficulty of this pattern is, however, that the establishment of the universal Communist society is posited as the final synthesis, the implication being that there are no further stages in the sequence distinguished by Marx: Asiatic, ancient, feudal, bourgeois, communist. Once the new millennium has arrived the theory of the dialectic loses its dynamism. History, so to speak, comes to a dead end, and an attempt at a 'scientific theory' of historical movement is displaced in favour of the dogma of a new apocalypse, a secular millenarism.

The dramatic impact of Marx's theory upon socialist movements of his time and thence forward was not the result of any widespread philosophical interest in, or acceptance of, the grandiose pretensions of dialectical historical materialism. What Marx's contemporaries and a multitude of disciples seized upon so avidly was rather the specific application of Marx's theory of historical movement to the phase of bourgeois capitalism which Marx and Engels characterized in terms of nineteenth-century Britain and Germany. What Marx and Engels appeared to offer to those men caught up in the surging tide of industrialization was an attractively simple explanation of past, present and future of their own society. For the wage labourers in the new-born industries, characterized by Marx and Engels as the suffering and exploited proletariat, they provided a compensatory reassurance. The ever-increasing antagonism and ultimate polarization of the proletariat and their exploiters, the bourgeois capitalists, was to lead to the ultimate certainty of victory for the revolutionary proletarian movement. Furthermore, this victory was not simply guaranteed as the result of the workers' own endeavours: it was predetermined by the fatal inner contradictions of the capitalist system itself. Best of all, the overthrow of the capitalist exploiting class, their ruling class ideology and their power structure, did not entail a retrogression in technology or the loss of the social benefits of the capitalist method of production. It was a doctrine of unstoppable modernization culminating in an age of universal abundance. In the utopia of the new communist 'true democracy' the exploitation and alienation inherent in bourgeois capitalism was to be finally swept away and the meek were to inherit the earth.

The main lines of Marx's theory of the origins, development and ultimate victory of the proletarian revolution are boldly sketched in the *Manifesto*. Many commentators have chosen to stress the passionate moralism of Marx's championship of the oppressed and his denunciation of the exploiters. It is perhaps appropriate to remind ourselves of the second-hand nature of Marx's images of oppression. His sources were primarily Engels' *The Conditions of the Working Class in England* (based on Engels' first-hand experience of industrial poverty and slum conditions in Manchester), and press and official reports. From this basis Marx created a hideous caricature of the oppressive bourgeoisie, a picture recalling the diabolism and conspiratorial theories of history characteristic of medieval sects:

> The bourgeoisie, wherever it has got the upper hand, has put an end to all feudal, patriarchal, idyllic relations. It has pitilessly torn asunder the motley feudal ties that bound man to his 'natural superiors' and has left remaining no other nexus between man and man than naked self-interest, than callous 'cash payment'. It has drowned the most heavenly ecstasies of religious fervour, of chivalrous enthusiasm, of philistine sentimentalism, in the icy water of egotistical calculation . . . In one word, for exploitation, veiled by religious and political illusions, it has substituted naked, shameless, direct, brutal exploitation.[17]

Nevertheless, the *Manifesto* proclaims, bourgeois capitalism contains the seeds of its own destruction, the symptoms of which are serious depressions and crises of overproduction. Such a system is 'like the sorcerer, who is no longer able to control the powers of the nether world whom he has called up by his spells'.[18] Because the conditions of the capitalist system become too constricting to contain the wealth they have created, the bourgeoisie struggles to postpone its own self-destruction by means of periodically destroying part of the productive forces, or by the conquest of fresh markets.

It is the revolutionary proletarian movement, however, that Marx and Engels envisage as aiming the death blows at the bourgeoisie. Because the capitalist phase of production is designated as the decisive penultimate stage in the development of the classless society, Marx and Engels envisage the revolutionary movement of the proletariat as the decisive movement. Avineri makes this point: 'Only because he sees in the proletariat the contemporary and final realization of universality, does Marx endow the proletariat with a historical significance and mission.'[19]

So eager was Marx to universalize the concept of the proletariat that he conveniently ignored the fact that, even within Western European countries, the industrial proletariat constituted only a minority of the population at the time he was writing. Indeed, Marx says: 'All previous historical movements were movements of minorities, or in the interest of minorities. The proletarian movement is the self-conscious independent movement of the immense majority, in the interest of the immense majority.'[20]

For the active leaders of the growing working-class movements, and for their middle-class supporters, sympathizers and would-be champions, the attractions of Marx's bold theories were immense. And despite the enormous volume of words Marx and Engels produced elaborating the 'scientific' pretensions of their theory, their discussions of their labour theory of value, and Marx's own closer analyses of the functioning of the capitalist system, neither Marx nor Engels were prepared to renounce or rescind the basic propositions of the *Manifesto*. In their later writings they proudly endorse the *Manifesto* and commend their critics and misrepresenters to return to it.[21] Furthermore, it is likely, as MacRae has pointed out in an illuminating essay,[22] that in an age characterized by the ever-increasing prestige of the physical and natural sciences, the use of a social scientific language and framework endowed Marxism with a certain glitter and attraction for the intellectuals.

A more tangible source of Marx's appeal to socialist movements was his determined and passionate internationalism, the conviction (constantly reiterated, for example, in the *Manifesto*) that the working-class struggle was a class struggle against a global capitalist system. Therefore the revolutionary conflict, though nationally based in its initial stages, is conceived as a world-wide struggle: hence the insistent injunctions to all Communist and socialist parties and movements to co-operate internationally, to adopt international strategy; and hence the practical efforts, from the International Working Men's Association onwards, to promote the International as a supra-national co-ordinating organ for the proletarian movement.

Socialist movements, seeking durable organization and effective political power, soon found, however, that there were real difficulties involved in harnessing Marx's theories to their needs, difficulties which derived from the inner-contradictions of Marx's theories.

Thoughtful working-class political leaders as well as middle-class intellectuals were equipping themselves with sufficient of the new knowledge of man, nature and society, to be able to challenge or question the validity of Marx's basic hypotheses. Marx thought of himself as the Darwin of the social sciences, but what if his claims to have discovered 'the economic law of motion of society'[23] and his whole grandiose apparatus of dialectical materialism and the labour theory of value, were built on false or inadequate premises? Most damaging of all, Marx's theories made firm predictions and aroused expectations that they would be fulfilled. It is true that the apocalypse of the international proletarian revolution and the utopia of the classless society could be projected safely into the hazy future. When, however, the predicted polarization of class conflict and the visible weakening and collapse of advanced capitalist industrial systems failed to materialize, it became increasingly difficult to explain this failure away.

It was not merely the impact of the searching and critical intellectual debate that began to undermine Marx's dogmatic claims to the status and authority of scientific truth. The historical experience of human irrationality on a grand scale, particularly in our own century, and the consequences of national pride, imperialist competition, racial conflict, hatred, discrimination and aggression, made Marx's 'truths' seem, at best, dangerously misleading half-truths. Marx's theory of history and, in particular, his projection of the development of class conflict under capitalism may be seen as an inversion of Manchester School economic theory, an inversion which preserved and, indeed, *hinged upon* the economists' assumption of rational maximizing individuals.[24] Marx's theory, because of its dogmatic historical materialism and bold comprehensiveness, utterly failed to grasp the importance of the irrational drives in human behaviour. Its pre-Freudian innocence made it increasingly unacceptable to Western intellectuals in the early twentieth century, to whom it came to appear as a rather naive reductionism. Among working-class movements the scientific pretensions of Marxism have been rendered increasingly obsolete by the experience of two shattering world conflicts which the theory neither predicted nor explained, and by developments in both Capitalist and Communist societies which appear to falsify Marx's prophecies.

For movements heavily influenced or guided by the theoretical inheritance of Marxism there are, moreover, two major sources of potential inertia. First, it is always open to critics or factions within a movement to disagree over their interpretation of the dialectic of the historical movement. After Marx's death to whom should the working-class movement turn for direction? Who was to say, at a given moment, that the conditions were ripe for revolutionary conflict, and that revolutionary consciousness was sufficiently developed to lead the proletariat to a successful revolution?

Second, Marx's dialectical materialism implied that the role of the individuals' contribution and influence was expendable. If the ineluctable forces of the dialectic of historical movement guaranteed ultimate victory, what was the use of individual action and endeavour? It was temptingly easy to argue, in situations where working-class political leadership and militancy were illegal and dangerous, that men should bide their time until conditions were 'ripe'. For the intellectuals, it was more comfortable to devote themselves to polemical factional disputes of the revolutionary *salons* than to risk the blood and pain of civil struggle and the barricades. Marx's own career demonstrates the basic contradiction in Marxist theory between the dialectic and the eschatology. Marx remained convinced that the revolution was bound to occur 'soon' yet he drew back from involvement in any concerted effort at a revolutionary seizure of power.

It is therefore not surprising that men of action, revolutionary leaders such as Lenin and Mao-Tse-tung, though inspired by Marx's language and vision, were compelled to resolve these contradictions. Drawing on the authority derived from their charismatic leadership *they* determined by fiat what particular revolutionary conditions, timing, strategy and tactics were to be applicable to their movements, and to their revolutions. Revolutionary Marxist-Leninist movements have tended to emphasize the apocalyptic, messianic, millenarian, anti-intellectual elements in Marxist thought. Their selective distortions and vulgarizations of Marx's ideas are woven into the creeds of surrogate religions aimed at the illiterate masses. Avineri states the point concisely:

> The implications of Marx's theory called for a proletarian movement. But the intellectual achievements of Marx's philosophy cannot provide without modifications an ideological basis for a political movement possessing organizational continuity and experiencing the normal ups and downs of political life. The vulgarization of Marx's theory thus becomes a necessary component in the make up of Marxist historical movements.[25]

Thus, although Marx's attempt at a science of historical movements has been generally discarded, some of his vision and moral passion, and his language, has been appropriated by bastardized Russian and Asian Marxisms—secular religions of mass movement. It is in this vulgarized form, and in contexts entirely unforeseen by Marx, that students of social movement find the clearest evidence of the continuing influence of Marx's thought as a source of constitutive values.

3/Typology and Politicization

In the first chapter an attempt was made to formulate a working concept of social movement distinguished in terms of: 1. conscious commitment to change, 2. minimal organization, and 3. normative commitment and participation. This working concept is closely linked with the concept of 'culture', defined as 'a whole way of life, material, intellectual and spiritual',[1] and with 'historical tendencies', for social movements both initiate and reflect changes in the wider society. The major advantages claimed for this broad conceptualization are its flexibility and cultural interchangeability. However, the very generality of the concept raises real difficulties when one attempts to typologize social movements. On what basis can the daunting variety of phenomena embraced by the concept be differentiated and categorized?

Historically, social movements are multi-dimensional and kaleidoscopic. British socialism, for example, has from time to time, contained the characteristics of a class movement, a quasi-religious labour sectarianism, a moral and intellectual crusade, populism, and even imperialism and nationalism.[2] The fact that its class movement dimension has usually been predominant should not mislead us into ignoring the other important dimensions, all of which exert a particular influence and require analysis and explanation. Thus also the Nazi movement at its zenith had a wide range of bases of support: for example, nationalism, imperialism, racism and anti-Semitism, lower-middle-class discontent and an appeal to youth. It cannot be adequately characterized as a counter-revolutionary conspiracy.

There is an ideological symmetry in Marx's attempt to categorize every movement in terms of the social conditions prevalent at the movement's inception. For Marx, every social movement is defined in terms of the prevailing method and social relations of production: every movement is seen as a class movement, and as an expression of class interest and class conflict. There have, of course, been formidable arguments raised against Marx's procedure of projecting the concept of class backward in time to pre-industrial societies, and against the enforced reductionism involved in a class typification.[3] Moreover, Marx's theory of class is singularly inadequate for the historical analysis or typology of phenomena such as religious, nativistic, nationalist or intellectual movements. To recognize this is not to deny the significance and value of the Marxist stress on the importance of material social conditions in the historical interpretation of movements.

The use of criteria such as the degree of ideological or organizational coherence or size of following as the basis of a movement typology has been rejected in the first chapter. It is, of course, possible to distinguish certain movements by the distinctive categories of the population to whom they appeal, or by whom they are supported. But there are many movements for which such a procedure would seem entirely inappropriate. Indeed, religious, millenarian and moral crusade movements frequently set out to *transcend* the narrow bases and constraints of class, sectional or national interest. Their ideologies, belief systems and patterns of normative commitment are therefore based on absolute, transcendental values of a religious or quasi-religious nature.

What, then, has what the Marxists like to term 'bourgeois social science' to offer by way of typologies of movement? A certain school of American political science has preoccupied itself with the development of a conceptual and theoretical framework for the study of extra-parliamentary and extra-party groups. Such an approach inevitably confronts, head-on, the problems of movement and group typology. David Truman, a well-known contributor to this approach, which is sometimes referred to as 'analytic pluralism', has admitted that 'no consensus of group theory exists'.[4] Yet in spite of the confusion and crudity of much political science 'group theory' it has been frequently utilized, if only because of the absence of any more sophisticated and viable framework. A brief critical discussion of this literature is therefore relevant here.

The antecedents of modern American group theory are English and German pluralism of the nineteenth century, which stemmed from the emphases of jurists (such as Gierke and Maitland) and of political theorists (such as Figgis) upon the role and influence of non-governmental associations in state politics. However, it is in the work of the American, Arthur F. Bentley, the founding father, in a sense, of modern analytic pluralism, that we find the most influential political science formulation of a group theory approach. In his *The Process of Government* (1908) Bentley defines the group as 'a certain portion of the men of a society, taken however, not as a physical mass cut off from other masses of men, but as a mass [of] activity which does not preclude the men who participate in it from participating likewise in many other group activities'.[5] Bentley claims that each group can be defined in terms of its 'group interest'. He conceives 'interest' as the group members' normative commitment to a claim or claims made by the group upon other groups in the social system. He sees the social system as a complex network of groups in dynamic interaction. Using the group as a basic unit of analysis, Bentley's theory of politics propounds that 'the push and resistance between groups' is the 'motor' of political change, and that the state of a society at a given time is equivalent to 'the balance of the group pressures'.[6]

There are clearly important limitations implicit in such a deceptively simple theory. It is ideologically and culturally limited in its applicability because it is assumed that all groups will accept a subsystem role in a plurality of groups; that each group will perceive its role as the winning of concessions against other groups in the process of group conflict; and that groups will conduct that conflict according to rules of the game which preclude, for example, an attempted revolutionary overthrow of the pluralist system.

Even in terms of its applicability to Anglo-American democracy the theory encounters serious logical and historical objections. It is extremely doubtful whether most militant members of interest groups (in any case a minority of the population in the US or UK) do attach such primacy to group loyalties or group interests. Indeed, there are strong grounds for assuming that the logic and ideology of atomistic individualism acts as a very effective counterweight to ideologies of collective action. Anthony Downs' conceptualization of the maximizing individual voter may reflect the US citizen's perceptions more accurately than group theory, for many citizens certainly do not look to any specific group leadership to mediate between themselves and other groups, or with governments. The corollary is that many citizens look to party leaders and government policy makers directly rather than to interest group mediation for decisive political authority and action.[7] Group theory was, in fact, historically initially a reaction against the jurisprudential formalism of nineteenth-century political science and, despite serious conceptual difficulties, the approach continues to attract US political scientists, perhaps because of its stress on the dynamics of political process.[8]

Among scholars working in the field of empirical pressure group studies the rife confusion over group concepts and terminology has been a severe handicap in developing typologies of groups. LaPalombara attempts to confine the interest group concept purely to organizations concerned with public policy.[9] S. E. Finer[10] prefers to use the umbrella term 'lobby' to cover all kinds of groups concerned with policy in the broadest sense, consultation and legislation, and he distinguishes two main types, the sectional interest group and the promotional group. Another study of British pressure groups by Stewart divides groups into two categories, those which have major demands and those which 'merely seek to escape the minor frictions that exist and which government intervention can either ease or decrease'.[11] Here also, as in Finer and other writers, the 'sectional' and 'cause' group typification is employed.

Conscious of the shortcomings of the 'group' concept in political science, Almond and Coleman in *The Politics of Developing Areas* (1960) attempt a more comprehensive and flexible typology which they clearly require for the comparative analysis of the interest articulation and interest aggregation functions derived from their structural-functionalist framework. They classify groups into 'institutional groups' (for example, military officer cliques, sections of the clergy or the bureaucracy), 'non-associational groups' (for example, kinship, tribal or other particularistic groups), 'anomic groups' (for example, rebellious, revolutionary or protest movements), and 'associational groups' (for example, purpose-rational bargaining associations of employers or trade unionists).[12] The basis of this typology is clearly the organizational form of the group, and the variety of 'styles' in which they articulate their interest. The joker in the pack is the 'anomic' group: the pejorative label indicates the author's implicit value judgement that these are essentially pathological or abnormal groups.* Such groups are dissatisfied with the political system and the bargaining and negotiating posture of the associational groups. The latter are accordingly designated as 'system functional', or superior groups

* Anomie (*or* anomy) is defined by *Webster's Seventh New Collegiate Dictionary* as: 'a state of society in which normative standards of conduct and belief are weak or lacking; *also*: a similar condition in an individual commonly characterized by disorientation, anxiety, and isolation.'

which properly 'maintain the boundary' between the political and social systems. The inappropriateness of such a typification to totalitarian systems or to African or Asian states, for example, hardly needs emphasis. Almond and Coleman, far from extending and adapting the group concept for the purposes of comparative analysis, appear to have oriented their typology to an ideal type of 'modern' or 'advanced' representative democracy.

Even in terms of its applicability to the USA, UK or Scandinavian polities, Almond and Coleman's classification is open to major objections. In the first place it is too static: some revolutionary groups or resistance organizations are temporary alliances or coalitions of 'institutional' and 'associational' groups. In other cases 'associational' leadership groups decide to resort to protest and extra-legal activity. By so doing they do not cease to be 'associational', and they may simultaneously pursue bargaining and negotiating tactics, with a government, for example, while resorting to extreme sanctions against another group. Secondly, it is an inadequate typology in that it fails to distinguish the very diverse types of associational groups, some of which have no immediate concern or involvement with public policy whatever. If one is going to discount such movements or groups then the group typology should distinguish them from other associational groups in some way.

An English political scientist, Francis Castles, has made an interesting, ambitious attempt to sketch a group concept and typology of greater comparative validity. He decides to use the term 'pressure group' as an umbrella term despite objections that the word has 'pejorative implications', and defines a pressure group as 'any group attempting to bring about political change, whether through government activity or not, and which is not a political party in the sense of being represented, at that particular time, in the legislative body'.[13] Unfortunately, Castles does not clarify what he means by political change, though he clearly means it to include pressure 'to change the government, and indeed the form of government'.[14] He therefore allows that, for example, nationalist movements must be included in his definition of pressure groups.

Castles' definition, however, runs up against the limitations implicit in the use of pressure group as a type concept in isolation, that is, without carefully interrelating it to the type concepts 'party' and 'movement'. No recognition is given to the fact that many social movements have, simultaneously, organizational forms and roles both as pressure groups and as political parties; that some political parties which gain legislative seats may be exclusively based on sectional or interest group organization and support (e.g. farmers' candidates in the USA, Canada and Scandinavia, or trade union candidates in France and Italy). Moreover, Castles' pressure group concept lacks comprehensiveness and flexibility as it explicitly excludes the many groups which are committed to change other than political change but which have important long-term political implications (e.g. birth-control movements, the ecumenical movements of the churches, experimental education movements, cultural-linguistic revival movements, etc.). The social movement concept covers a much wider range of collective endeavours and is not so culture-bound as the pressure group concept. Accordingly, I wish to argue, the pressure group is best understood as a specific organizational form of social movement. It does not constitute an adequate basis for a typology of collective action.

The bases for the typology of social movements adopted here are derived from the defining characteristics of the social movement. Some movements are best defined by the character and implications of the commitment to change or changes adopted by the movement, others by their organizational mode and strategy, and others by the 'constituency' of the population which accords the movement normative commitment and participation.

In the typology we shall adopt, each category is purely an ideal type, and, as with all such taxonomies, the typology requires qualification. It is most unlikely that any particular social movement can be accurately categorized in terms of only one ideal type. For example, Martin Luther King's civil rights movement in the USA was part moral crusade, part reform movement, part religious movement, as well as being a campaign for racial equality. Moreover, each type frequently embraces a wide range of organizational forms. For example, nationalist, class, reformist and revolutionary movements may find expression in fully fledged political parties, pressure groups, trade unions, conspiratorial societies, or in youth, women's or cultural organizations, or in any combination of these. I shall adopt the following main types or dimensions as a framework for the present discussion:

1 Religious movement, millenarism and sect
2 Movements of rural and urban discontent

3 Nativist, nationalist and race movements
4 Imperialism and pan-movements
5 Class and occupational interest movements
6 Moral protest and reformist movements
7 Revolutionary, resistance and counter-revolutionary movements
8 Intellectual movement
9 Youth movement
10 Women's movement

Using this typology certain key aspects of social movement will now be examined: first, the complex subject of the origins and sources of different kinds of movement and of the social, economic and political conditions which constitute the most fertile soil for such movement; second, the analysis of varying patterns of movement ideology, leadership and organization; third, theories and models of movement development; finally, there is the theme of movement politicization. The problem of politicization, or the degree to which movements acquire a political character and relevance, is obviously germane in a series designed to cater to the needs and concerns of political scientists. It is true, as Heberle insists, that almost all social movements have political implications. (Heberle, 1968.) Yet, however broadly we choose to define political activity, it is clear that some movements will have more profound and far-reaching political implications than others.

In order to talk meaningfully of degrees of politicization it is necessary to distinguish the political from other forms of activity. The definition of *political activity* I propose to adopt is derived from both distributive and historical approaches to the problem of political power: it is not my intention, therefore, to impose an inappropriately rigid, scientistic definition of power. As Mackenzie has forcefully pointed out,[15] the historical experiences of varieties of political power range along a very wide continuum. At one end, one encounters societies in which power may be experienced entirely through verbal persuasion and the emergence of consensus. Such societies blend into others whose governmental structures rely on traditionally accepted, legitimated authority, and those in which material inducements and governmental or bureaucratic influence are valued sources of power. At the other end of our continuum lie those societies whose governmental structures depend for their power predominantly upon their possession of a monopoly of coercive powers, upon the threat to use these powers against challengers to their authority, or upon the frequent use of their coercive powers to bludgeon or terrorize the population into submission.

For the purposes of the present discussion, I shall define political activity as that embracing any action involving the distribution and utilization of power within a state, social collective or corporate group. Such activity may include: critical discussion of existing distributions and utilizations of power; advocacy and actions in favour of a radical redistribution of such power; argument and actions directed towards the abolition of all governmental, associational or corporate powers; and pressures for the utilization of such powers for novel, or hitherto unaccepted, purposes.

Any study of the conceptual and empirical discussions of social movement does underline the fact that systems analogies and metaphors derived from natural and mechanical sciences fit, at best, extremely awkwardly in this field. One cannot avoid the fact that, historically, social movements are multi-dimensional, seamless and constantly in flux. Most evince a simultaneous combination of activities: political, religious, economic, recreational and so on. All effective social movements, even some extremely short-lived ones, may have political implications in that they must be taken into account in the political activities of governments and individuals.

Furthermore, I wish to argue that it is short-sighted to focus all our attention upon what might be called primary-level politicization among social movements. One is unnecessarily restricting one's view of politics and foreclosing possibilities of extending one's insight into political change, if exclusive attention is given to those movements which have acted directly through political party or pressure group organizations. It is tempting to concentrate on those movements that have consistently engaged in mass demonstration, lobbying, civil disturbance, rebellion, resistance, etc. Such activities provide incontrovertible evidence of politicization. It is therefore not surprising that political scientists have extensively drawn upon, and contributed to, the literature on class, revolutionary and protest movements.

In the ensuing review and analysis, I hope to show how more indirect, long-term cumulative effects of other social movements can be of fundamental importance. (They may be, indeed, as significant as the factors extensively analysed by political sociologists of development such as S. M. Lipset and Barrington Moore,[16] who concentrate on social structure, social mobility, patterns of industrialization and urbanization.) For example, religious and moral crusade movements such as Christian missionary movements or the anti-slavery movements have had incalculably more profound long-term influence in the shaping of society and politics than many of the more obviously political movements that have scrambled for political office or representation.

4/Religious Movement, Sect, Millenarism

What distinguishes the religious movement or dimension from other movements? If we attempt a rigorous definition of religion we risk losing ourselves in the quicksands of philosophical debate. In its most general sense 'religion' embraces all prevalent systems of faith and worship past and present, an almost infinite variation. Not all movements or ideologies have achieved the status of a religious system of faith and worship. Is there any common denominator shared by those that have?

Their first major characteristic is that they lay claim to a source of doctrinal authority which transcends the individual. This source need not necessarily be conceived as a supernatural personification or power. 'Religion without revelation'[1] may be grounded upon abstract principles, a doctrine of history or a supreme political ruler.

H. J. Blackham in his interesting work *Religion in a Modern Society* (1966) distinguishes four major forms of religious interest: ecclesiastical religion or the traditional cults and faiths, rituals and practices; political religion, that is to say creeds and doctrines legitimating systems of political authority; cultural religion, by which he means a rational search for 'the knowledge and techniques for a comprehensive art of life';[2] and popular religion which may take the forms of popular superstition and paganist propitiation of evil spirits, popular myth, popular millenarian or apocalyptic sectarian movements, or 'religions of the oppressed'.[3] As Blackham points out, ecclesiastical religion may frequently set out to cater for the needs of popular religion: he cites the Roman Catholic tradition of assimilating and 'baptising' paganisms. Also, in the case of political religion, society and the state may be integrated in a theocracy, or an ecclesiastical religion may be exploited for political purposes. An entirely new political religion may be introduced to replace traditional religion, as in the case of the Soviet Union or Mao's China. Clearly, movements may arise in any one of these religious spheres or 'interests', or in any combination of these forms. Moreover, we must not assume that any one of these religious forms is more genuine or enjoys more intense normative commitment than any other. The follower of a political religion, such as a militant supporter of the Communist party, is just as capable of fanaticism and devoted self-sacrifice to his cause, as the Jesuit or the Jehovah's Witness are to theirs.

This brings us to the second key distinguishing characteristic of religion, and that is its capacity to reorient radically individual personality and behaviour. The individual believer or follower feels himself compelled or 'bound', 'as a duty' as Weber put it, to believe and to act in accord with his religion. In the religious movement above all others, the individual convert is subjected to powerful moral pressures to alter his behaviour, his whole way of life, in accordance with his new-found normative commitment.

Third, an obvious and important feature of religion is its claim to primacy and to authority on the basis of its monopoly of revelatory or rational ideological truth. Because of this quality, religions are inevitably to a greater or lesser degree mutually disjunctive in a world of rival religions. It is as well to be aware of this assertive, combative, conflict-inducing and revolutionary potential of religion which counter-balances those 'integrative capacities' which numerous sociologists and anthropologists, following Durkheim, have sought to emphasize. S. F. Nadel, for example, in his *Nupe Religion* (1954), considers religion's 'competence to hold together societies and sustain their structure'[4] to be one of its major capacities.

The fourth feature, religion's power of promoting social integration and solidarity, deserves some amplification. Clearly, religion and religious movements often tend, whether by accident or design, to help in the reinforcement and conservation of social cohesion and discipline, to underwrite a prevailing social structure and pattern of authority. Religion may perform this conservative role in a number of important ways. It can reinforce leader identification and group identification and reverence for tradition among its adherents. Religious symbols and rituals can provide drama, poetry and stimulation, and a socially controlled safety-valve for the expression of potentially violent and disruptive passions such as fanatical devotion, envy or hatred. Most fundamental of all, religion can and often does provide an ultimate moral basis and sanction for the normative codes of society: for example, in the West, Christianity provided a grounding of natural law on which the positive law of the state could be based.

Whether seen from the point of view of its revolutionary or its conservative role, the importance of religion as a factor in social change is such that it is difficult for any grand theorist of society to evade. The foremost problem of any sociology of religion (as distinct from a religious sociology) is to determine the degree of autonomy and decisiveness which can be attributed to religion or religious movement in sociological analysis. How far can religious belief and practice *per se* determine the direction, shape and pace of social change?

Marx had an acute sociological perception of the importance of religion. He wrote: 'Religion is the general theory of this world, its encylopaedic compendium, its logic in popular form, its spiritual *point d'honneur*, its enthusiasm, its moral sanction, its solemn complement, its general basis of consolation and justification.'[5]

Yet Marx repeatedly forecloses further debate of the problem of the historical role of religion by his dogmatic assertions that religion is both a social product and an illusion. He declares in his introduction to his *Kritik des Hegelschen Staatsrechts*: 'Religious suffering is at the same time an expression of real suffering and a protest against real suffering. Religion is the sigh of the oppressed creature, the sentiment of a heartless world, and the soul of soulless conditions. It is the opium of the people.'[6]

It is not surprising that Marxists have been unable to make any serious contribution to the sociology of religion. Religion is seen by them at best in terms of primitive and obsolescent folkways; at worst it is castigated as an insidious ideological weapon of the exploiting class. It becomes necessary to abolish it. Traditional religion must be replaced by revolutionary ideology and revolutionary consciousness: 'The abolition of religion, as the illusory happiness of men, is a demand for their real happiness. The call to abandon their illusions about their condition is a call to abandon a condition which requires illusions'[7] (i.e. the abolition of capitalist exploitation).

In contrast to Marx, it is the great strength of the three classic pioneer exponents of modern sociology of religion (Max Weber, Émile Durkheim and Ernst Troeltsch) that they do not ideologically foreclose the exploration of the complex relations between religion, society and social change.

Ernst Troeltsch published the results of his enormous effort to develop a historical sociology of Christianity in *The Social Teaching of the Christian Churches* (1931). Troeltsch accepted that it was primarily the poor and oppressed to whom Jesus preached and among whom the early Church won most of its new urban adherents. Nevertheless, Troeltsch argued that the core problem in early Christian literature and the New Testament itself is always essentially religious: 'This "Hope of the Kingdom" was not a promise of revolution in another existence: it was primarily the vision of an ideal ethical and religious situation, of a world entirely controlled by God: values of redemption were purely inward, ethical and spiritual.'[8]

Troeltsch became convinced that the Christianity of the early Church was a distinctively religious movement. It could not be explained as simply the social product of a class struggle or national rivalry: it was not the *direct* result of any general social and historical trends. Troeltsch did agree that many of these external factors *indirectly* prepared the way for an era of creative religious experience coincident with the period of Roman imperial decline. He cites the following major determining factors:

1 The destruction of national religions that had resulted from the loss of national independence.
2 The intermingling of races and cults.
3 The rise of mystery religions stressing the importance of the inward life and transcending limitations of nationality and birth.
4 The fusion of various fragments of religion which had broken away from their national foundations.
5 The growth of a philosophical religion of culture (e.g. among the Hellenes) which in various ways became assimilated into the popular religions.
6 The world empire's need for a world religion.
7 An extraordinary growth of deeper and more spiritual ethical thought.
8 The rise of polytheism, and the accompanying desire for a definitive universal religion.

What is especially arresting about Troeltsch's analysis is that most of the *indirect* influences he identifies are primarily religious factors:

> Only those who see in all spiritual movements merely the influence of social movements [Troeltsch means 'class' movements here], and especially those who imagine that all

> religion is merely the reflection of social conditions in transcendental terms, will see in them a direct cause of the religious crisis . . . to some extent at least, religious thought is independent; it has its own inner dialectic and its own power of development . . .[9]

Max Weber is similarly confident concerning the autonomy of the religious factor:

> However incisive the social influences, economically and politically determined, may have been upon a religious ethic in a particular case, it receives its stamp primarily from religious sources, and, first of all, from the content of its communication and its promise . . . wherever the direction of the whole way of life has been methodically rationalized, it has been profoundly determined by the ultimate values towards which this rationalization has been directed. These values and positions were thus *religiously* determined. Certainly, they have not always, or exclusively, been decisive: however, they have been decisive in so far as an ethical rationalization held sway, at least so far as its influence reached. As a rule, these religious values have been also and frequently absolutely, decisive.[10]

I shall now turn to the rich and extensive literature of the history and sociology of religion, and in particular to that concerned with the major religion of the Occident, Christianity. This literature, following the courageous example of Weber, has vigorously attempted to interpret and analyse religion on a global scale and I certainly cannot do justice to this large area of religious studies. Nor have I the necessary knowledge, space or justification for extending this discussion into anything approaching an adequate exposition of the classic sociologies of religion as such.[11] The object of this short introductory typological review is to identify within this literature certain key concepts, themes and theories which have a specially direct relevance to theories of religious movement development, leadership, organization and politicization. Many of these concepts and theories, moreover, have a potentially wider applicability to the general analysis of social movements. Indeed, some writers set out to construct a general theory of social movements on such foundations, as does Weber with the concept of charisma.

Charisma

Max Weber derived his famous conceptualization of charisma originally from the work of Rudolf Sohm, who pioneered its clarification in his study of the early Christian Church, *Kirchenrecht*. The strict religious usage of the term charisma denoted a gift of grace or spiritual endowment possessed by an individual and derived from divine or supernatural sources. Weber broadened this definition considerably by applying it to:

> A certain quality of an individual personality by virtue of which he is set apart from ordinary men and treated as endowed with supernatural, superhuman, or at least specifically exceptional powers or qualities. These are not accessible to the ordinary person, but are regarded as of divine origin or as exemplary, and on the basis of them the individual concerned is treated as a leader.[12]

Weber held that, for example, military or hunting leaders or politicians could possess charismatic qualities as well as religious leaders or prophets. He categorized leadership based on charismatic grounds as one of the three most important types of legitimation of authority. Its basis was 'devotion to the specific and exceptional sanctity, heroism or exemplary character of an individual . . . and of the normative patterns or order revealed or ordained by him'.[13]

In the religious context Weber regarded the prophet as the prototype of charismatic leader. There are two essential preconditions for genuine prophecy, Weber argues. First, the leader must challenge the established normative order both by proclaiming a break in that order and by declaring it to be morally legitimate. Second, and equally vital, 'It is recognition on the part of those subject to authority which is decisive for the validity of charisma. This is freely given and guaranteed by what is held to be a "sign" or proof, originally always a miracle.'[14] The prophet, of course, does not regard his legitimacy as being dependent on this recognition. In his eyes it is the compelling moral duty of the people to follow him even if this commitment is formally voluntary. Prophets are distinguished from priests by the direct and personal character of their call and of the doctrines and commandments they derive from their revelations. Weber claims, 'It is no accident that almost no prophets have emerged from the priestly class.'[15] (Weber's assertion that Luther, Wesley, Calvin and Zwingli, for example, were not prophets because they did not claim to be speaking in the name of a divine injunction is, incidentally, flatly contradicted by detailed studies of the lives and doctrines of these men.[16])

Far more serious objections may be found against Weber's elaboration of the theory of charisma and its 'routinization' as a theory of social movement and institution building, both at the religious and the general level. He distinguishes the following general characteristics of the pure type of charismatic authority:

1 Charismatic authority, in contrast to bureaucracy, does not evince orderly structures, appointment, dismissal, or career training and 'management' and has no formal agency of control or appeal.
2 The 'success' of the charismatic leader in performing his 'mission' decides whether he will receive obedience and a following.
3 Charismatic authority of the 'pure type' is inherently opposed to rational economic conduct and ordered economy and is not primarily interested in pecuniary gain.
4 Leader and disciples, in order to perform their task, avoid worldly ties, routine employment and family responsibilities.
5 'Charismatic domination means a rejection of all ties to any external order in favour of the exclusive glorification of the genuine mentality of the prophet and hero. Hence its attitude is revolutionary and transvalues everything . . . [The charismatic leader will proclaim] It is written, but I say unto you.'[17]

Weber says remarkably little about the socio-psychological origins of charismatic devotion, though he does stress the importance of man's needs for cosmic meaning and for saviours offering roads to personal salvation. Rather, he takes the existence of charismatic leadership as given, and then explores the implications of charisma for social change.

He emphasizes that charismatic leaders can endow both their followers and the social organizations they establish or sustain with some of their charismatic power. The emergence of the charismatic group and the routinization of charisma are one and the same process, and institutionalization of charisma whether of office, kinship, heredity or 'contact' necessarily develops as the charismatic leadership attempts to preserve continuity of succession. Weber's hypothesis is that the charismatic beliefs, doctrines and symbols tend to become more and more firmly assimilated, especially in the religious and political institutions of society, until the charisma becomes fully 'routinized'.

Such 'routinization' at the level of ideology or values is augmented by the powerful processes of rational socialization and the emotional neutrality and standardization inherent in *rational discipline*. The charismatic leadership of the Jesuits or the Bolsheviks, for example, paradoxically cannot impose its will without the agency of strict, uniform discipline (e.g. the Jesuit Order, CPSU or Red Army) which inevitably tends to routinize the movement's charisma.

Weber sees, then, the emergence and assimilation of charismatically derived goals and norms as a constant and normal aspect of social change. S. N. Eisenstadt, an extremely sympathetic commentator on Weber, goes further and argues that 'the development of such charismatic personalities or groups constitutes perhaps the closest social analogy to mutation, and the degree of their ability to forge out a viable symbolic and institutional order may be an important factor in the survival or selection of different societies or cultural creations'.[18]

The stress on the role of the individual charismatic personality of the leader brilliantly elaborated by Weber does provide us with a valuable concept and an insight into an important aspect of social movement which is obviously not limited in its applicability to religious phenomena. It gives us a useful denotation and framework for analysing the problem of leader-follower relations in social movement. To determine the extent to which such a framework can be generally applied to social movement we need to know more about the *sources* of charismatic authority. How far are they socially, ideologically and historically derived (whatever the leader's claims to originality)? Does the emergence of the charismatic individual *always precede* the development of a movement? May it not be the case that a genuinely collective or communal relationship between a small or large number of individuals frequently initiates and sustains a movement, especially in cultural-historical contexts where collectivism is the norm?

A contemporary sociologist of religion, Werner Stark, voices some of these doubts in criticism of Weber's charisma theory. Stark has argued, in connection with the early Catholic Church, that organization and charisma, priest and prophet, were co-existent and interdependent right from the earliest stages of the growth of early Christianity. He objects that Weber's dichotomy is entirely misleading, especially when applied to a church such as the Catholic Church which although of ancient origin still attempts to preserve that collectivism. For Stark, institutions in such circumstances have as much reality and genuineness as individuals, a reality which is ideally and effectively communicated through the agency of the sacraments and the succession of the priesthood. If Professor Stark is correct, then we must recognize the limitations of the charisma theory in its general application to all religions and social movements.

Theories of religious development

1 *Rationalization.* Weber conceives of religious phenomena evolving through stages of gradually increasing rationality. At the substantive level, this involves greater clarification of religious ideas, more abstraction in the method of posing problems, and greater complexity and systematization of doctrine. At the functional level, greater rationality involves more complex patterns of normative control and sanction, and a more systematic organization of religious practice. Weber saw this broad evolutionary pattern as a general tendency. He did not make the error of assuming that irrational beliefs or movements magical, demonic or constrictive in character would entirely disappear, though it can be argued that he underestimated the possibilities of the re-emergence of powerful movements of an irrational character.

In *Religionssoziologie*[19] Weber elaborates his comparative historical analysis of the rationalization process. Weber holds that there are a number of 'directions' and 'paths of development' which can lead to a 'breakthrough' from the primitive religious state. At moments of decisive crisis there is a choice to be made between evolutionary religious change which will not involve radical change in the established order and a more drastic kind of change. The prophets are the crucial agents in the process of 'breakthrough' to a more rationalized form of religion.

It is important to note that Weber's 'evolutionary' conception of religious development does not entail a predetermined ultimate withering away of religion. Rather he envisages an unending process of religious refinement and modification. Only in his conception of *Entzauberung*, or demystification, does Weber suggest the possibility of a general process of secularization which would ultimately render religious movements obsolete.

Weber's recurrent theme, however, is that in any society, whatever the character of a specific normative order, there will always be a discrepancy between the expectations derived from the normative order and individual experience. This discrepancy will be all the more deeply felt in the case of a highly rationalized religious system. When people experience suffering or evil which the religion cannot prevent or explain, then, Weber argues, individuals will seek to resolve the problem by finding saviours who offer them the prospect of personal salvation and a meaning for human existence.

2 *Sociological determinants.* Weber claims that, although there is no uniform pattern of sociological determinants in the case of religious movements, it is generally in times of despair and distress that prophets and preachers will find the readiest followers. The alienated urban population of the ghetto or slums, the poor, the unemployed and the rootless are therefore more amenable to the appeals of religious movements than the more traditionalized peasantry or the political and military élites who have a vested interest in the established order. Weber does not imply that peasants are necessarily immune from the influence of prophetic or religious movements. He argues strongly in chapter 6 of *Religionssoziologie*, however, that, with a few minor exceptions,[20] peasants were never important as carriers of rational ethical religious movements in the later development of Judaism or in the rise of Christianity.

Christianity was, he argues, essentially an urban religion from the beginning. He argues that urbanization is in itself an important sociological determinant of the form of the Christian religion. An organized congregational religion could only develop out of the life of the city in which taboo barriers between clans had been transcended and there was 'the concept of the community as an institution, an organized corporate entity serving specific realistic functions'.[21]

Weber is in agreement with Troeltsch in his insistence that religious movements have not been *primarily* movements of economic protest or simply a means of kicking against the pricks by the underprivileged or oppressed. Like Troeltsch, he shows that various bourgeois and intellectual classes have played very important parts in the rise of religious movements.

Troeltsch, in a brilliant exposition, seeks to explain the contrasting effects of differing social bases upon the character of cultural-rational and popular religious movements:

> New religious movements of this kind develop along two lines: on the one hand they proceed from the rarefied atmosphere of cultivated thoughtful circles, and express themselves in criticism and speculation; their actual importance depends upon the depth of the real religious vitality which these forms of criticism and speculation conceal. Platonism and Stoicism, each in its own way, are examples of new religious movements of this kind. Essentially, however, both are systems of reflection and attempts to reach truth through the reason, and therefore they never achieve the specifically religious power of a faith founded on revelation. Conscious of their weakness, they cling in part to the old popular religion, which they merely explain in somewhat different terms, and in part they base their confidence on the power of the abstract arguments which each individual may construct for himself after quiet reflection on the explanations offered by these systems. On the other hand it is the lower classes which do the really creative work, forming communities on a genuine religious basis. They alone unite imagination and simplicity of feeling with a non-reflective habit of mind, and primitive energy and an urgent sense of need. On such a foundation alone it is possible to build up an unconditional authoritative faith in a Divine revelation with simplicity of surrender and unshaken certainty. Only within a fellowship of this kind is there room for those who have a sense of spiritual need, who have not acquired the habit of intellectual reasoning, which always regards everything from a relative point of view. All great religious movements based on Divine revelation which have created large communities have always issued from circles of this kind.[22]

3 *Denominationalization of sects.* Ernst Troeltsch pioneered the use of the church/sect typification in the sociology of religion. In broad terms 'church' denotes those ecclesiastical and religious

organizations which are broadly supportive of an established cultural and social order, while 'sect' denotes a group which rejects, to some extent, the wider society. It is extremely important to distinguish the sociological from the historical usage. Historically 'the Church' denoted a community which transcended all national and territorial bounds and indeed all earthly limits, a total Church with absolute authority not only over religious matters but also, at the peak of its medieval power, over temporal affairs. Any deviation from, or rejection of, this authority in the religious sphere was denounced as a schism, an apostasy or a heresy. From the heretic's point of view very often the established Church was guilty of apostasy or was seen as the servant of the Antichrist, the betrayer of the true religion. Though the sociological usages of church and sect are fairly neutral and avoid the value-loading of religious propaganda, the typification has been made the basis of a somewhat reductionist and therefore unsatisfactory sociology of religious development.

H. Richard Niehbuhr in *The Social Sources of Denominationalism* (1929) and Liston Pope in *Millhands and Preachers: A Study of Gastonia* (1942) elaborate the theory that there is an inherent tendency towards accommodation or deradicalization in the development of sects. As sects become routinized and institutionalized they tend, so Pope and Niehbuhr argue, to compromise with the established order, to accept their pluralist situation, and to increase in respectability, organizational complexity and wealth, to the point where they become 'denominationalized', part of the plurality of mutually tolerated churches.

This thesis has been forcefully and convincingly rejected by Bryan Wilson in *Patterns of Sectarianism* (1967). He challenges the assumption that all sects have a basically similar ideology, social composition, organization and pattern of development. Wilson argues that while some sects and religious movements *do* become denominationalized others do not and he seeks to analyse the reasons for the *persistence* of sects. This issue has extraordinary relevance for the general theory of social movement because the assumption of the inevitability of movement deradicalization has been used extensively (as will be seen in chapter 7) in theories of revolutionary political movements.

Wilson distinguishes certain common sectarian characteristics, among which are exclusiveness, self-perception as an elect, acceptance of the ideal of the priesthood of all believers, a high level of lay participation, and a more clearly defined ideology or creed.

These contrast with the distinctive features of a denomination, among which Wilson includes 'openness', breadth and tolerance, vagueness and ambiguity on doctrinal matters, the use of a trained ministry, and a more restricted use of lay participation. He attempts a classification of sects and religious movements on the basis of varying responses 'to the values and relationships prevailing in society'.[23] 'Conversionists' (e.g. Salvation Army and Pentecostal sects) try to alter the world through converting men. 'Adventists' seek to prepare for a new millennium whose arrival they predict (e.g. Jehovah's Witnesses). 'Introversionists' seek to replace worldly values of the individual by higher inner values (e.g. Quakers). 'Gnostics' adopt various kinds of mysticism as an instrument for attaining normal worldly goals (e.g. New Thought, Christian Science).

Introversionists and adventist sects and movements, Wilson argues, have proved to be the best insulated against denominationalizing tendencies. Sects which are most subject to denominationalization are those which have a democratic ethic, accept simple affirmations of 'conversion' as a qualification for admission, engage in vigorous evangelism and seek to assimilate groups disrupted by social stress or crisis.

However, Wilson's most cogent point against the simple denominationalization theory is that the earlier studies (Troeltsch, Niehbuhr and Pope) overlooked the distorting effects of special historical circumstances upon patterns of sect development. For example, it was, he suggests, external factors (such as rapid social change, high social mobility, intensive immigration and urbanization) which largely explain the extraordinarily accommodative denominationalizing sequence of sect development in the USA after 1800. In other cultural-historical contexts this rate and scale of denominationalization is inconceivable, and sectarian survival and persistence are frequent alternative patterns of development. It is interesting that Wilson's critique of the denominationalization theory brings us back to the importance of a more complex interaction of historical and sociological determinants.

Of course there is a very real possibility that the denominationalization theory contains a more serious misunderstanding of religious development. Should we assume that denominationalization of a sect invariably involves a decline of commitment, a loss of spirituality, energy or creativeness? Is it not possible that a movement of internal renewal may rejuvenate a church even in a pluralist situation? Further, in the light of recent evidence of progress towards ecumenism, at least among Protestant churches, is it not possible that denominations may find a way of reunifying and recreating a genuinely transcendent and universal church?

4 *Secularization.* Strictly speaking, secularization is not simply a theory of religious development. The term can be applied to a sweeping hypothesis about religion and society; in simplest outline it assumes that all religious ideas, beliefs, practices and organizations will wither away under the impact of positivistic and empiricist ideologies of science, technology, management and social engineering. The fully secularized world will be one in which man has won complete control over himself, when all religious claims can be confidently relegated to the history books, and when churches can be opened as museums or converted into welfare clinics or play-centres.

As might be expected, Marx looked forward with confidence to the fruition of secularization:

> The religious reflection of the real world can, in any case, only finally vanish when the practical relations of everyday life offer to man none but perfectly intelligible and reasonable relations to his fellow-men and to Nature. The life-process of society, i.e. the process of material production, will not shed its mystical veil until it becomes the product of freely associated men, and is consciously regulated by them in accordance with a settled plan.[24]

Some professing Christians such as Harvey Cox in *The Secular City* and Paul van Buren in *The Secular Meaning of The Gospel* have gone so far as to welcome this prospect of 'total' secularization and have attempted to interpret this as a master process in which God somehow intends or wills man's total 'liberation' and separation from religion. Thus there is a point at which secularization as a theory of history merges into what David Martin and Leslie Paul correctly identify as ideologies of secularism.[25]

The obvious point to be made about the hypothesis of general secularization is that only *global* historical experience over centuries will confirm its truth or falsity. I do not wish to engage in the voluminous ideological debates about how far the rise of Christianity itself has, as Harvey Cox has suggested,[26] initiated and promoted the secularization process. Historically it must not be denied that the Reformation and the rise of Protestantism in North-western Europe and North America dramatically hastened the process of political secularization, i.e. the increasing separation of church and state, which was already well under way in Catholic states of the Renaissance. It is true, again particularly of Protestant states, that the extent of secular control over such spheres as education, culture, diplomacy and administration widened enormously at the expense of the Church. The rise of toleration within the predominantly Protestant states with their plethora of sects and denominations ensured the establishment of a religious pluralism in which no single church, whatever its legal or doctrinal claims, could enjoy a monopoly of religious control, however vehemently it asserted its title to be the one true church. In Catholic states, of course, the Church fought a long and bitter rear-guard action against political secularization, state education and religious pluralism. It certainly succeeded in limiting or, at least, greatly retarding, these secularizing tendencies in predominantly Catholic countries.

Furthermore, it is true that the figures of regular attendance for religious worship among all major British denominations over the past fifty years do show a steady decline. But it would be a parochial view to regard this as convincing evidence for general secularization. A decline in religious *belief* does not follow from a fall in attendance. And even if church-going in Britain fails to recover markedly, there is still the remarkable vitality of United States church attendance to be accounted for. Moreover, we must not neglect the constant and often frenzied recurrence of what Blackham calls 'popular religions' of folk-culture, 'pop-idol' worship, hippie cults and so on.

And what of Asia and Africa? China has witnessed the development of a powerful new mass political religion in the shape of Maoism. In South and West Africa the movements for independence were frequently accompanied by a bizarre profusion of messianic, utopian and millenarian movements. Holas has described, for example, the astonishing vitality and spirituality of a Liberian catechist's movement—Harrism—which partly inspired the emancipation movement in the Ivory Coast.[27] In the Nigerian Civil War a prophetess and her cult were widely credited with bringing about a collapse in morale in a key front-line regiment. In Africa such religious movements—many of them exotic, ephemeral, almost unknown to the Western intellectuals—are an enormously influential and significant phenomenon.[28]

Further evidence of the unsatisfactory character of the general secularization hypothesis is to be observed in the phenomena of millenarian movements which Vittorio Lanternari has termed 'religions of the oppressed'. These revolutionary religious movements continue to exert a strong attraction for the poor, the rootless, the disinherited, the alienated, caught in the distress and despair and the sense of personal loss and confusion engendered by rapid social change.

Millenarism

Lanternari uses the term 'messianic' to describe the religious cults or movements of salvation deriving from the revelations of prophets or guides whose doctrines point the way to salvation. Others describe them as 'chiliastic' movements, preferring this synonym for the belief or believer in the millennium. 'Millenarian', however, now has the broadest consensus of acceptance among social anthropologists and historians concerned with these phenomena and this provides some justification for adopting the term.

What these movements have in common is their revolutionary promise of the advent of an age of bliss, abundance and perfect justice. In a narrower, earlier meaning, the millennium meant the ushering in of a literal thousand-year reign of Christ on earth, but we must not assume that such eschatologies and revolutionary chiliasms are uniquely associated with Christianity. Lanternari notes that certain millenarian prophecies and messianic cults appear to have arisen in societies completely isolated from Western colonizing influences and missionary Christianity, though there is a regrettable lack of data about such movements. It should also be noted that Professor Norman Cohn in his classic study of medieval revolutionary chiliasms, *The Pursuit of the Millennium*, does not claim that such movements are exclusively phenomena of the Judaeo-Christian religious tradition.

Nevertheless, as Professor Cohn persuasively and eruditely demonstrates, the Jewish and early Christian traditions are the richest and most important source of millenarian phantasies and movements. He finds the original source of such prophecies in the monotheism of the Jewish religion, the belief in a God not only of the Jews but of history, and the belief in their historical role as the 'chosen people'. The hardship, tyranny and humiliation suffered by the Jewish people was seen repeatedly as both a punishment and a test of their fitness for the final triumph which their Lord God would ultimately bring to them. Ultimately God would bring his people out of Egypt into the paradise of the 'promised land'. These chiliastic visions were intensified with the rise of Christianity and 'generation after generation was seized at least intermittently by a tense expectation of some sudden and miraculous event in which the world would be transformed, some prodigious struggle between the hosts of Christ and the hosts of Antichrist through which history would attain its fulfilment and justification'.[29]

However hard the official ecclesiastical authorities tried to stamp out the apocalyptic tradition, it continued, in various forms, to recur in popular religions of the early Middle Ages. Cohn argues that it was in the period between the eleventh and early sixteenth centuries that revolutionary chiliasm came into its own as a dynamic social myth and as the driving force of mass movements. He suggests an explanation for this. He finds that it is primarily in situations of rapid social change, urbanization, population expansion and economic disruption or dislocation that millenarian movements exerted their revolutionary appeal. They occurred typically, therefore, not in traditional settled peasant farming regions, but in the expanding new cities and areas of early industrial development such as the Rhine Valley, Holland, Bohemia, Westphalia and London.

It was in such centres that newly arrived immigrants from the countryside had their eyes opened to the opportunity of rapidly acquiring new wealth, security and status in craft or business. Other men's success seemed to prove that poverty and dependence could be overcome. There was accordingly a revolution in expectations at a time when only a few could satisfy their wants. It was therefore among the poor, the unemployed, the frustrated, the beggars and the rogues that millenarian movements found their readiest audiences.

The examples detailed by Cohn show both the continuity of the apocalyptic pattern of prophecy and some of its more bizarre and violent manifestations. The prophet Tanchelm emerged as leader of a popular movement against the Church in early twelfth-century Brabant, Utrecht and Antwerp. He preached that the clergy served the Antichrist and churches were no better than brothels. His followers were told to abstain from the Church and its sacraments. They fêted Tanchelm like a king and some drank his bathwater as an alternative to the Eucharist!

In addition to the bizarre and fantastic qualities of revolutionary chiliasms, Cohn's study stresses the violent and destructive effects of their frequent political interventions. In the first years of the twelfth century, for example, the fruits of the *prophetae* who preached the First Crusade were the poor deluded unprepared hordes who followed such men as Peter the Hermit across Europe. Entirely ignorant of the real difficulties that faced them, fanatically, often hysterically, devoted to the cause of the hour, they were frequently inspired more by the chiliastic desire to reach and capture Jerusalem than to aid Christian Byzantium. These hordes were beyond the control of the military and ecclesiastical leaders of the Crusade. The wildest and most terrifyingly violent element of the *pauperes* were the *Tafur* whose very name put fear into the hearts of the Crusader and Moslem armies alike. The *Tafur* are a salutary reminder, if one is needed, that mass barbarism and savage violence have not been the prerogative of the twentieth century. This 'army' of ill-kempt and lice-ridden ex-beggars and bandits armed themselves with knives, sticks and clubs, and were not above cannibalism. Not only did the most violent of the hordes loot, pillage and rape the captured territories of the Crusading War, but they turned also against the envied and often prosperous Jewish communities of their own cities, such as Speyer and Mainz, in the first large-scale massacre of European Jewry. There were moreover, as Cohn notes, elements of bitter class hatred in the wider clashes of the later Middle Ages between chiliastically oriented mass movements of the urban poor and the wealthy urban oligarchs.

Cohn argues that revolutionary millenarisms have their psychic origin in a form of group paranoia. He claims that the irrational fantasies of such movements appeal to individuals prone to paranoid states of mind. Such individuals tend towards a megalomaniac delusion that they are special or divinely chosen persons, inclining to ascribe all evils to a diabolic conspiracy and hungering for a reign of saints and a perfect world. In short, Cohn proposes a psycho-pathological explanation for the mass appeal of millenarisms to the disoriented, disturbed and insecure, and for the evident fanaticism and savage determination which they evince in their quest for 'final solutions'. It may be agreed that Professor Cohn's characterization of the paranoid style of millenarian movement, and his suggested explanation of them, appear especially convincing when applied to the medieval chiliasms he investigates. It is interesting, however, that in his search for other cases of the paranoid style of millenarism he comes up with only two clear-cut comparable instances: the rise of the totalitarian mass movements, Nazism and Bolshevism, in their revolutionary heyday.

Certainly it is easy to identify certain millennialist elements in both Nazi and Bolshevik doctrines. Both proclaimed that there would be a final struggle against the forces of evil which would be won by the 'chosen people' (whether the Aryan 'master race' against the Jews* and foreign capitalists or the proletariat against the bourgeoisie and all reactionaries). It is assumed that the victors will be amply compensated for all the hardships and sacrifices they endure by attaining the 'perfect society' (whether this is seen as Third Reich or universal Communism). But, of course, recognition of such elements is not sufficient to provide an adequate characterization or theory of totalitarian movements.

And if all revolutionary movements cannot be understood purely in millenarian terms, certainly one can also show that the view that all millenarisms necessarily involve mass violence and appeals to a group paranoia is seriously mistaken. Certain movements which have placed very great stress on the creation of a 'new society' have been entirely pacific in their activities and have based their doctrines purely and simply on a rational analysis of social development. This type of millenarism characterized many of the *Philosophes* in their visions of the future, outstandingly in the writings of Condorcet. And, to take another example, the Owenite movement has been convincingly characterized by the historian, Professor Harrison, as constituting basically a millennialist sect throughout its history with the exception of the short period of Owenite syndicalism in the early 1830s.[30] One can find relatively recent survivals of this form of rational millenarism in Britain in the utopian socialist sect run by H. G. Wells and C. E. M. Joad in the 1930s, the Federation of Progressive Societies and Individuals with its Enlightenment-style journal, *Plan*.

Undoubtedly the richest contemporary source of religious millenarian movement development is to be found in those Third World cultures which have most recently experienced the traumas of colonial occupation and withdrawal and the disruption and dislocation of indigenous cultures which has normally ensued. There is a huge and fascinating anthropological literature on these

* Nazism, in common with many medieval chiliasms, directed its propaganda of diabolism and its barbarous persecutions primarily against the Jews.

phenomena.[31] Such movements range from the North American Indian Ghost Dance and buffalo cults which taught that the colonial rule of the white man would be ultimately destroyed and the Indians restored to their rightful dominion,[32] to the Melanesian cargo cults described by Peter Worsley's important study *The Trumpet Shall Sound* (1957). The Melanesian cargo cult movements expect their ancestors to return to them to liberate them from colonial rule, and to bring European inventions and products for their use. In preparation they have set up landing strips, storehouses and 'wireless masts' which are of purely decorative value. Almost invariably such movements are anti-colonial and the millennium they await is liberation from foreign rule. Worsley explains convincingly why primitive societies tend to develop millenarian movements. Such societies, he argues,

> . . . lack advanced technology and scientific knowledge. The people are ignorant of the findings of advanced natural science . . . They have little power either to predict the onset of natural disasters or to control or counteract them . . . These deficiencies in scientific knowledge and practice . . . provide ample room for the elaboration of fantastic explanations in animistic or other supernaturalist terms. The primitive peasant is thus predisposed to the acceptance of supernaturalist interpretations of reality.[33]

In Worsley's analysis, millenarian movements are most likely to develop in the following situations: in stateless societies where the people have no political structures available to them (i.e. no bureaucracy, no police, no military force); among the poorest classes in agrarian and feudal societies; when a society's political leadership is consistently defeated in the course of its struggle for survival; or when the political leadership fails to answer the people's needs.[34]

Lanternari, in a most useful comparative analysis of Third World millenarisms,[35] stresses the role of imperialism in inducing the growth of chiliastic and messianic cults: it both attempts to socialize the native populations it controls, and awakens the native peoples to their own economic backwardness or deficiencies. He also makes the extremely pertinent observation that the millenarisms of the Afro-Asian cultures have borrowed very extensively from the evangelism and messianic imagery of Christianity. Citing examples among Kikuyu, American Negroes, Maoris and Bantu, he notes how such people have found their own fates and sufferings reflected in the biblical history of the Hebrew people. In the Bible they found in the stories of David, Jacob and Solomon, 'religious justification for the polygamy of the natives, which the missionaries had so violently condemned'.[36] More important still, they found a rich and inspiring model in the life and sacrifice of Jesus Christ for a doctrine and promise of salvation which could be readily applied to their own native prophets and hopes and struggles for political liberation. The 'verandah boy' movement in Ghana not only sang hymns to their hero Nkrumah, but also their propoganda portrayed the governor as Pontius Pilate and their leader as Jesus Christ. Among the underprivileged masses of Latin America, icon-like portraits of Ché Guevara and Fidel Castro increasingly appear, complete with halos, alongside the Christian iconography. Popular revolution becomes repeatedly and inevitably transfused with popular religion, and they are most powerfully and effectively combined in a doctrine of millenarian promise, a hope of spiritual and earthly salvation. The millenarian element or dimension of religious movement is likely, therefore, to be of continuing and vital significance both in the developing world of the 'have-nots', and in every situation of severe social stress such as economic collapse, national humiliation in military defeat or severe internal conflict.

Political relevance

What general conclusions can one draw about the political implications and politicization of the various forms of religious movement? In the course of our brief review of key concepts and forms of movement which are important concerns of the literature, a number of factors emerged which have an implicit political relevance. My aim here is simply to highlight and examine briefly the most salient of these factors.

The first and most fundamental general factor is the important and largely autonomous capacities of religion as a determinant of large-scale social change. This is the overwhelming conclusion not only of historical studies, but also, as we have seen, of the classic contributions to the sociology of religion. It is the besetting weakness of theorists who hold that universal secularization is inevitable that they can see every religious movement only in terms of a grand dialectic of decline. Thus revivalism is seen by them as a pathetic attempt to rejuvenate a dying religion or denomination, an attempt foredoomed to failure because, in their terms, it is against the grain of history.

Historically, the evidence of the pervasive influence of religion upon ethics, social institutions, morality, family life, and indeed the whole shaping of political legitimations, is overwhelming. Even in the most technologically developed 'secularized' Western societies, the legal-institutional forms, public rituals, symbols, imagery, the general culture and the educational process, all mediate values and ideas derived from the Judaeo-Christian religious tradition. It is true that this tradition has met stiff opposition from movements proclaiming an aggressive anti-clericism and atheism, but the churches have been fighting this ideological battle at least since the Enlightenment. In fact, it is probably the case that we now tend to underestimate rather than overestimate the formative influence of religious tradition in Western societies, just as we may overestimate the significance of the role of Oriental religions in their social contexts.

To take one example, consider the transformative capacities of Lutheran and Calvinist Protestantism which so interested Weber and Tawney[37] in their studies of the dynamics of economic and social change. In his careful analysis of the recent interpretative debate on the Protestant ethic thesis, S. N. Eisenstadt[38] concludes that, despite considerable modifications needed in the light of fresh evidence, Weber's and Tawney's broad thesis concerning the transformative capacities of Protestant ethical orientations is sound. These capacities certainly contributed, in combination with political-technological factors, to the rapid commercial expansion of post-Reformation Europe. Among these transformative capacities of the ethic most accounts stress the prime importance of Protestantism's 'this-worldly' involvement, its central concern with the individual's direct relationship with God and with God's word unmediated by any sacramental and priestly institution, and its emphasis upon the importance of individual initiative and responsibility.

Again, if one examines the religious movements and conflicts of the late eighteenth century it becomes clear that, as Professor Harold Perkin cogently argues,[39] they did express to a considerable extent the latent class antagonisms of the developing industrial society. But of course they were far more than lightning-conductors or surrogates for class conflict. They exerted a positive and distinctive social influence. The rise of Methodism is a case in point.

Methodism, with its democratic organization, its stress on lay participation and leadership, and its commitment to service and co-operation in the wider society, was in a real sense the prototype of a modern democratic mass movement. Its chapels, preaching organizations, and day-to-day management provided a superb training ground for voluntary association and leadership, a rich source which radical, trade union and co-operative movements were to draw upon liberally throughout the nineteenth century.

Far more radically transformative or disruptive social influences are the revolutionary millenarisms of the type which Cohn describes, with their propensity for collective paranoia and violence. In circumstances of extreme social stress such chiliasms can attempt a revolutionary seizure of power or provoke civil war.

At the other extreme, one must consider the effects of social inertia which ensue from the conservatism of a traditional ecclesiastical religion enjoying a monopoly of religious authority. How could one explain the demographic history, economic development, or the political nationalism of Ireland, without reference to the role of the Roman Catholic Church?

It is helpful to conceive of *direct politicization* of religion and religious movements, in the sense defined in chapter 3, as a two-way process.[40]

First, there are the attempts of political leaderships of all types to penetrate, influence or manipulate religious collectivities in order to serve their own political purposes. Whether the justification for doing this is couched in elaborate religio-ideological terms or is simply grounded on *raison d'état*, the attempt at control involves two factors: the recognition of the powerful hold of the religious institution or movement over a large section of the population by virtue of the strength of normative religious commitment; and a political calculation of the most appropriate strategy, resources, leverage or inducements to adopt in the quest for political control. The theocratic model of ancient Egypt and, at certain periods, ancient Israel, is probably of comparative historical rarity. In such cases it is hardly relevant to speak of a process of politicization, for in their absolute form such systems institute a political caste which is coterminous with the priestly class. Far more common in the history of Western church-state relations is the use of outright corruption, bribery, patronage or simony, all practices at which the Borgias, Henry VIII of England and Louis XIV of France, for example, were notoriously adept. In their dealings with the Catholic

Church the European rulers traditionally employed two other important types of control or restraint. The first was encouragement of politically convenient doctrinal parties and theological interpretations and the suppression of uncongenial or potentially politically weakening rival factions. (Hence, Louis XIV was happy to make use of congenial elements of the Gallicanist movement in French Catholicism which accorded well with a policy of independent national aggrandisement, while he suppressed or restrained, often with great ruthlessness, the politically inconvenient Jansenist and Ultramontane elements within the Church and the Huguenot 'heretics' beyond it.[41]) The second was employment of diplomatic and military power for the purposes of blackmailing or manipulating Church authority, for imposing specific clerical or papal nominees, extracting favourable rulings and privileges, and generally abusing the dependence of successive popes upon the temporal diplomatic and military protection of princes.

Like the absolute monarchs before them modern dictators have not, in any instance, been able to claim total success in their attempts at the political subjugation of religion. It is true that Franco, Mussolini and Hitler managed to secure a period of relatively passive co-operation from the established church leaders, and that in the Soviet Union the remnant of the Orthodox priesthood was beaten into submission to the state after the Church had suffered severe repression. Yet in none of these cases did the dictatorship succeed in totally eliminating all sources of religious resistance, moral and active. Priests have repeatedly been associated with the illegal workers commissions in Spain, and with campaigns for civil and economic rights. In the cases of Hitler Germany and Communist Russia there is a long and well-documented[42] tradition of religious resistance, particularly on the part of devoted minority Protestant movements who have discovered the realities of martyrdom and sacrificial service for their beliefs.

The reverse process of politicization occurs when religious organizations, movements and sects attempt to translate their beliefs into direct social and political action. Here are some of the means most commonly used:

1 Frequent intervention directly as a social welfare agency both providing and administering relief services, either in times of war or natural disaster or when the political

leadership either refuses such provision, or has inadequate resources to provide for the social welfare.

2 Involvement in international and national 'pressure group' activity, lobbying, mediating and recommending specific policies.

3 Formation of their own parties and trade-union movements, or acquisition of existing ones, to promote their aims.

4 Attempts to influence the politically legitimating values and political socialization of the young through educational work, the maintenance of religious schools, and the work of brigades, church youth movements and other youth auxiliary organizations.

5 Involvement in revolutionary resistance.

Thus the multi-dimensional character of social movement is admirably illustrated by the phenomena of 'colonization' of religious movement by political leaderships, factions or groups, and by the enterprising and varied repertoire of political strategies and tactics which religious organizations have initiated or utilized in order to influence, reform or radically transform society.

5/ People, Nation, Race and Empire

Rural and urban movements

'Popular movement' is too broad a term to constitute a type of social movement in any meaningful sense. 'The people', surely, are the vital *matériel* of all social movements. Should we not therefore concentrate on discovering which categories of people have supported which movements and under what conditions? These are indeed important questions to ask about every kind of social movement, and to a large extent the quality of movement analysis depends upon the accuracy and comprehensiveness of the historical and sociological evidence marshalled in the attempt to answer them. There is, however, a need for a separate residual category of social movement to accommodate the often ephemeral and frequently turbulent movements of rural and urban popular discontent. Indeed when historians talk of 'the people' they generally mean the 'common people', the 'masses', the poor and the underprivileged. Such movements and risings of the poor, so often equated with 'the mob' or 'the rabble' have a history which is probably as old as permanent human settlement. The slave riots and city risings of antiquity and the peasant revolts of the Middle Ages, such as the violently destructive *jacquerie* in France between 1357 and 1358, are all part of this ancient tradition.

Some scholars have chosen to designate such phenomena as essentially 'primitive' or 'archaic'.[1] It would perhaps be more circumspect to avoid designating popular riot and protest as archaic phenomena for there are plentiful examples of explosive and destructive food riots, incendiarist mobs and machine-breaking attacks (and not only in Third World countries) in the mid-twentieth century.

It is extraordinarily difficult to analyse and explain extremely short-lived and turbulent outbreaks even with all the modern aids of television documentary coverage, police records, press film, depth-interviews with participants and so on. Unimaginably more difficult is the task of social historians dealing with outbreaks of over a hundred years or more ago. Hobsbawm and Rudé highlight thc difficulties in their fascinating work of historical detection concerning the participants in the last English agricultural labourers' rising:

> Who were they? Nobody except themselves and the rulers of their villages knew or cared, nobody except the clergymen or (much more rarely) dissenting minister entered the few basic facts of their obscure lives in the parish register: birth, marriage and death . . . We know little about them, because they are remote from us in time. Their articulate contemporaries knew little more, partly because as townsmen they were ignorant about the country or cared nothing for it, partly because as rulers they were not allowed to enter the self-contained world of the subaltern order, or because as rural middle class they despised it.[2]

Clearly, on a global scale, a myriad earlier and later rural outbreaks have been entirely unrecorded. This is no longer due to any shortage of an able and ardent corps of professional historians willing to search for the remotest trace of a rising. It is because there are in many cases no traces left. Where a rising or riot produces no written programme, manifesto or ideology, and when its leaders are unknown, such anonymity becomes almost inevitable. Only when the authorities are sufficiently concerned to intervene, and attempt, normally with ruthless success, to suppress the disturbances, is there a strong likelihood that local or central government records will contain some passing reference to the occurrence.

It is useful at the outset to distinguish between isolated riots, risings or disturbances and those more durable and organized collective endeavours that have succeeded in sustaining a rural or urban protest movement over a period of months or years. There are a number of brief and tragic confrontations between crowds of poor, unarmed civilians and armed troops or police which enter the mythology of the revolutionary tradition. Peterloo, Father Gapon's March and Sharpeville, for example, have become powerfully emotive symbols charged with memories of popular heroism and martyrdom: they are saints' days of the revolutionary calendar. However, it is important that we do not confuse such phenomena as surging crowds, demonstrations, protest marches or riots with more stable, clearly delineated and durable social movements. It is historically more accurate to perceive such occurrences as frequently initiated and utilized by organized movements: for example, when the Jacobins made use of the Paris crowds (especially the turbulence and discontent of the *sans-culottes*), when the *communards* played on the grievances of the Paris National Guard, or when the Bolsheviks helped to foment and unleash the frustration of demoralized Russian troops in the 1917 revolution.

Short-term outbreaks of collective anomie—volatile and disruptive popular discontent—can, by their nature, never be entirely controlled. Every movement which has attempted to mould a popular ideology, to achieve mass support and mass participation, has attempted to subordinate and convert mass discontents to its own political purposes. In political revolutionary movements, once the immediate purpose of revolutionary seizure of power has been achieved, the turbulent and unpredictable revolutionary crowd is frequently perceived as a threat to the new order and it is often ruthlessly destroyed. So strong is the will of the leadership to conserve its monopoly of power that it may even turn its guns on the people who helped bring about the revolution, as was the case in the massacre of the *communards* or the crushing of the Kronstadt revolt. Revolutionary dictatorships outlaw all autochthonous expressions of populist discontent or protest. Mass participation will be restricted to the displays, parades and rallies that become agencies of the ritual and symbolic legitimation of the regime.

In the pluralist democratic tradition, radical popular democratic movement has not been historically homogeneous. All modern constitutionalist parties proclaim their belief in popular sovereignty as a fundamental principle, and perceive the people's right to universal suffrage as at once the expression and legitimation of democratic government. In Britain, for example, the reformers in 1867 and 1884 would appear to have won the battle for acceptance of the *principle* if not the substance of popular sovereignty: it was the culmination of a long and arduous campaign which had been courageously initiated by Tom Paine, the Chartists and radicals. Even among nineteenth-century Tories, Burkean aphorisms defining all power as a trust 'from the people and for the people'[3] were common currency as the party prepared for the vulgar expediencies of competing for popular support.

The secularization of politics occurs when it has become widely accepted that man's social relations, material conditions and destinies are amenable to positive, collective, secular endeavours and when it is no longer generally believed that all can be left to the hand of God and king. When the principle of popular sovereignty has been generally accepted and politics becomes, in addition, democratized to a considerable extent, it becomes valueless to talk in general terms of 'the people's movement', for all movements with any degree of mass support inevitably represent some of the people some of the time. The differing and fluctuating popular bases of nationalist, imperialist, class, reformist and revolutionary movements will therefore be considered later. There are, however, two types of phenomena which do fall into the general category of urban and rural discontent which we shall consider more closely. The first are the ephemera of city mobs and crowds, and the second the more durable movements of rural populism.

The theoretical and empirical literature on crowd phenomena is scant despite a recent acceleration of interest (see Smelser's *Theory of Collective Behavior* and Cantril's *Psychology of Social Movements* for valuable bibliographies and reviews of the classic literature). The tendencies of recent work in this field have been to emphasize and explore the relationship between outbreaks of collective violence and civil strife and wider social forces. Some see these disturbances as symptoms of rapid demographic and economic change, changes in expectations or relative material deprivation.[4] Other interpretations stress the importance of the development of ideologies of violence as an important contributory factor,[5] and there are many alternative hypotheses. The most serious lacuna exists in the field of detailed historical studies of the political roles and influence of mobs and crowds, particularly in major revolutionary crises. George Rudé's *The Crowd in the French Revolution* (1959) is a superb but almost unique pioneer attempt in this field and there is, regrettably, no equivalent attempt to deal with the crowd factor in 1917 Russia or at the fall of the Weimar Republic.

In a valuable essay,[6] E. J. Hobsbawm has analysed the role of the city mob in pre-nineteenth-century Europe. Such mobs 'developed a sub-political complexion'[7] of their own, rooted in the solidarity of the urban poor in ancient quarters, such as the Trastevere in Rome. These mobs oscillated between passive dependence on the monarch or prince of their city and riot when they became acutely dissatisfied with conditions. Hobsbawm equates this phenomenon with urban banditry. He sees mob violence as a desperate response of the poor when the ruler fails to provide the security, minimal livelihood or compensatory largesse which the mob expects from its governor. Hobsbawm emphasizes that up until the French Revolution such movements of the urban poor were rootedly legitimist. It did not occur to them to seek a revolutionary political order, for they saw their monarch as both a divine and a popular symbol, and as the embodiment of justice. Just as anti-clericals of eighteenth- and nineteenth-century France could remain passionately Christian in conviction, so the ancient city mobs blamed the king's officials rather than the monarch for their sufferings. The extent of the ideological impact of the French Revolution upon the character of popular movement can be gauged from the fact that by 1848, throughout Western Europe (though not yet in Eastern Europe or Russia) the city mob had ceased to be legitimist and had begun to align itself behind revolutionary movements and heroes.

The assimilation of these short-term phenomena into competing revolutionary and liberal democratic traditions has led inevitably to ideological conflicts in the historiography of revolution. Marxist historians have struggled valiantly to justify a clear-cut class definition of successive movements by reference to the social composition of revolutionary crowds. Such investigations, based largely on police reports and court-case evidence associated with disturbances, do not provide any simple proofs of the theory that class homogeneity and class grievances are the root determinants of such phenomena. In the case of the French Revolution, for example, both Soboul[8] and Rudé[9] have concluded that the *sans-culottes* were not a homogeneous social class. They constituted a political alliance of varied social origins including *rentiers* and civil servants as well as petty traders, shopkeepers, craftsmen and journeymen. Over one quarter of the civil *commissaires* of the Paris *sans-culottes* in the Revolutionary year II were property owners, most of them small property owners. If the movement was not a struggle of the unpropertied classes, what was its basis? What substance had the contemporary meaning of the term? We are left with Soboul's definition of the *sans-culottes* as a variegated *political* coalition reacting against privilege, landed wealth and seigniorial rights.[10]

The fact that Marxist-Leninist historians have given such prominence to the role of the *sans-culottes* in the French Revolution stems from the movement's affinities with Lenin's own revolutionary theory and practice. As Alfred Cobban has pointed out, 'Russia in 1917 and France in 1789 offer obvious parallels'.[11] Lenin was also attempting a political coup in a largely pre-industrial context. His chosen instrument, the élite revolutionary vanguard, was to *induce* externally the revolutionary consciousness which could not possibly have emerged spontaneously from the pre-revolutionary Russian workers, peasants and soldiers. What we have here is an interesting example of the crudely ideological character of much of the historiographic debate on the roles of popular movements. Whether one emphasizes and characterizes them in terms of economic motivation or political struggle should *not* be decided purely upon grounds of ideological preconceptions. Much more precise and compelling evidence is needed before class typifications of urban mobs (or crowds as Rudé prefers to term them) are made convincing.

Furthermore, we should not assume that the contemporary social scientist with his battery of survey techniques can simply resolve all the baffling problems of distinguishing the precise social composition of a crowd involved in a disturbance. Let us assume that our investigator has the sensitivity to popular feeling, and the inside knowledge of demonstration organizers' plans which would enable him to be present at the 'crucial' phenomena he wishes to study. Does he then bravely thrust forward into the throng armed with his questionnaire or tape recorder? By this time the crowd may have confronted police or troops and our investigator will quite possibly come between a demonstrator and a water-jet or between a policeman and a *pavé*. Moreover, he cannot evade this difficulty successfully by seeking co-operation from the police, by interviewing those unfortunate participants held for questioning. Will such a setting, and the suspicion of police collaboration by the interviewer, be conducive to a fruitful and open exchange of information? Moreover, by this method, probably only a tiny handful of the total crowd involved would be reached. Would our investigator be better engaged pursuing the birds who have flown to the safety of their lodgings?

One temptingly simple escape from these difficulties is the hypothesis that all crowd disturbances, riots, etc., are caused by agitators.[12] Less crude and more influential is the large psychopathological literature which attempts to relate the phenomena of mobs and movements in general to underlying patterns of psychological motivation and to anatomies of specifically authoritarian or fanatical personalities. Most well known of the recent accounts of the psychological syndrome of extremism are *The Authoritarian Personality* (1950) by T. W. Adorno *et al.*, *The Open and Closed Mind* (1960) by M. Rokeach and *The Social Psychology of Social*

Movements (1965) by H. Toch. Despite recent elaborations of terminology this mode of explanation is hardly new. In the eighth century AD Alcuin enjoined his readers, 'Nor should we listen to those who say, "The voice of the people is the voice of God", for the turbulence of the mob is always close to insanity.'[13] And in the nineteenth century Gustave Le Bon[14] based a general theory of crowd and movement behaviour on this basic assumption.

Le Bon used the term 'crowd' in a rather special sense: he meant not just a random collection of individuals but a group of persons dominated by the desire to achieve a specific object. Le Bon's definition appears to embrace only organized demonstrations, rallies, mass meetings, parades and marches, with a specifically political object. He asserts that a crowd's mentality is inferior to that of any average participant's individual mentality. It is irrational passion rather than rational thought that is expressed in the subconscious herd instinct of the crowd. Crowds are therefore able to carry out acts of extreme heroism and extreme bestiality and savagery which no rational individual would perform on his own.

Le Bon's psycho-pathological theory of crowd disturbances and protest movements emphasizes the role of rumours, hatreds, fears and superstitions, which sway the crowd, and the phenomenon of mass hypnosis by skilful leaders of movements. Not surprisingly, such a view leads him to conclude that crowds and mass movements are basically a diabolic influence. If unleashed they risk wrecking the civilization created by a small élite. They act, he writes, '... like microbes which hasten the dissolution of enfeebled bodies. The moment a civilization begins to decay it is always the masses that bring about its downfall.'[15]

Such immoderate condemnation is not stated so baldly in recent psycho-pathological literature, but a somewhat jaundiced and historically distorted view of movement is generally implied and this vitiates much of the analysis.[16]

There is an extremely interesting and analytically valuable literature on the more durable peasant and rural 'populist' movements of the nineteenth and twentieth centuries. The sporadic outbreaks of Hodge's rebellion described by Hobsbawm and Rudé in *Captain Swing* constituted a kind of embryo modern populism which has striking affinities with more recent and better documented movements. The English farm worker of *Captain Swing* was the victim of rapid proletarianization accompanied by severe economic crisis: 'He became not merely a full proletarian, but an underemployed, pauperized one, and indeed by the time of the 1830 rising he retained little of his former status except the right to parish relief, though even this was to be withdrawn from him within a few years.'[17]

Although he was a proletarian in the economic sense, he lacked the relative freedom and capacity for organization of the urban poor. As is so often the case with populist movements, the rural poor were especially constrained by the demands of their daily work and the hierarchical character of rural society. In common with later populists, 'Hodge' tended to maintain a stubborn political legitimism, a suspicion of new ideologies and programmes, and a simple conviction that his claims were lawful. There was a long delay before the full-scale development of unionism among the agricultural workers provided a more sophisticated and effective form of movement in the 1870s. Hobsbawm and Rudé suggest convincing explanations for this protracted period of 'archaic' populism among the English farm labourers. They argue that their economic situation was so poor that they could neither obtain some of the advantages of labour shortage nor pay union dues. Also, the rural workers were so demoralized and degraded by their dependence, the tradition of deference, and the callous way in which they were often treated by the landowners that they were afraid of forming unions. Furthermore, rural workers were unfamiliar with the principles of unionism which had developed in an urban industrial setting. One should also add that they were burdened by the illiteracy of the bulk of their members, and by the absence of a national railway network of relatively rapid centre-peripheral communication which facilitated the general development of unionism on a national basis.

Modern populism in Europe, Russia and the United States displays many characteristics of this earlier rural protest: a certain primitive xenophobia, intolerance, anti-urbanism and anti-industrialism. Although in America rural populism is frequently anti-intellectual, the European and Russian movements were partially inspired and encouraged by the intellectual romanticism of Rousseau, Herder and Tolstoy with their images of 'natural man' and ideals of brotherhood.

MacRae has succinctly explained (Ionescu and Gellner, 1969) the appeal of the populist syndrome to alienated groups of rural populations who feel threatened by modernizing and proletarianizing tendencies of industrialization. Populism does not offer such groups an elaborate ideology or indeed a comprehensive political programme; rather, it proclaims its faith in the essential virtues of the simple people and its suspicion of, or outright hostility towards, all élites. Typically, populist leaders portray all big city interests as part of a diabolical conspiracy to cheat and oppress the people. In order to defeat these demons and to recover a mythical golden age of rural bliss populists often espouse panaceas such as land redistribution or 'social credit'.[18] 'General' Jacob B. Coxey of Ohio, for example, who led the populist Industrial Army Movement of 1894 in the USA, developed a cure-all economic formula, in the form of a non-interest bond bill, to relieve unemployment and achieve public improvements. (Coxey, like all American populists, was obsessed by the need for freer credit facilities for the small farmer, and he later propounded a loan plan whereby local banks would grant loans on the security of goods and chattels, even on livestock, grain and raw materials.[19]) Paradoxically, populism frequently demands state intervention to resolve the economic difficulties of the poor, and yet such movements rarely develop stable and coherent political parties with specific policies which could make a determined long-term effort to take control of government.

In sum, rural populism represents a style of loosely-organized, ideologically ambiguous, anti-élitist and romantic movement. It lacks acute political consciousness, coherence or staying-power, and finds the language of religion and myth (for example William Jennings Bryan's fire and brimstone fundamentalism and William Aberhart's millennialism) more appealing than the language of politics. Not infrequently, other movements assimilate and politicize rural populisms. Populisms can thus become transmuted into more positive and assertive movements and their grass-roots supporters may become committed to more ambitious and comprehensive ideologies. By itself, however, populism remains, as one analyst has aptly expressed it, 'a syndrome, not a doctrine',[20] its movements expressing an alienation and a yearning for a rural age of abundance, feelings which are frequently exploited by revolutionary, reformist, nationalist and racial movements alike, with considerable effect.

Nationalist movements

There is no justification for restating the history of nationalist concepts and doctrines, as this has been outlined in several able accounts to which the reader is referred.[21] Nevertheless, students of social movement will note a lack of analytical and comparative studies of nationalist movement. It is therefore necessary to draw on some of the historical sources[22] for the purposes of characterizing and interrelating the major forms of nationalism.

Medieval Europe was innocent of modern doctrines of nationalism. Linked by the concept (if not by the reality) of a united Christendom and by the common language of the Catholic Church, the states of medieval Europe constituted parcels of dynastic inheritance. The boundaries of these empires, kingdoms and principalities were often ill-defined, and were drawn without regard for ethnic, linguistic or religious homogeneity. The kingdom was what the king could hold against the military and diplomatic rivalry of his competitors, and the king's subjects therefore maintained a kind of tripartite structure of loyalties: duty to the church (which was conceived as separate from, and transcending, temporal rulers), duty to the king and loyalty and service to the lord of their own locality. Often, the sovereign and the lord had to resort to coercion when loyalty or service was withheld. The term 'nations' had therefore no political significance until the late eighteenth century. It simply meant, as Kedourie puts it, 'groups belonging together by similarity of birth, larger than a family, but smaller than a clan or a people' or 'places of provenance'.[23]

The origins of modern political nationalism lie in the historical movements or trends in evidence in the Western European states of the sixteenth and seventeenth centuries whereby the loyalty to the king and the king's government became identified with, if not equated with, the overall interests of the ruler, his officials, and the entire population. Most important of all, when *raison d'état* and increasing cultural-linguistic identification were reinforced by the economically maximizing potentialities of mercantilist, centralized, state governments, the nation-state clearly emerged as the predominant and most viable European political unit.

The modern European political doctrines and movements of nationalism did not crystallize, however, until the French Revolution. It was, as noted earlier, primarily in the writings of Rousseau that we find the most powerful source of the recharging of the nation-state concept and the basis of nationalism as a political doctrine. Rousseau and the Jacobins asserted the claims of the *whole population* to sovereignty over their state, for the first time proposing that the model state was coterminous with the nation.

Principles of national solidarity, universal citizenship, equal rights to civic participation and equal treatment under the law, all underpin the modern doctrines of nationalism. Once defined in terms of the entire population within a given territory, or a whole ethnic or linguistic group, nationalism asserts that the nation should become the fundamental and universal unit of political organization. Human society becomes a world of nation-states. The inevitable corollary (revolutionary, of course, in the context of nineteenth-century Europe) was that any nation that was oppressed by another had the right to be emancipated and made fully politically self-determining so that it could enjoy 'full nationhood'.

The nationalist doctrine has been attacked very effectively on three main fronts. The first practical point raised is that there is no clear agreement about how the nation should be defined. Linguistic, ethnic and cultural-historical differences have an unfortunate habit of cross-cutting. The national determinationists in the Versailles settlement, for example, confronted ultimately insoluble difficulties in following this principle to its logical conclusions. Far from creating a new map of watertight 'pure' national units, the 1919 frontiers created fresh problems for the national minorities inconveniently trapped on the wrong sides of the new state boundaries.

Secondly, as Kedourie forcefully argues, the insistence of nationalists upon the right of national self-determination has often been mistaken by well-meaning Anglo-American liberals for a preference for constitutional democracy as a form of national self-government. Successive newly independent nation-states of the Middle East, Africa and Asia have shown that independence in no way guarantees the adoption and maintenance of democratic, free elections, parliamentary government, an independent judiciary or the protection of basic civil liberties in the state concerned.

The third point, which is the burden of E. H. Carr's brilliant short essay *Nationalism and After* (1945),[24] is that the spread of nationalist doctrines and movements has, far from creating a happy family of nations, exacerbated international conflict. Indeed, nationalist doctrines have provided additional justification for revolution and war, have formed the basis for a popular commitment to, and involvement in, national struggles, and have provided a powerful political rationalization and propaganda instrument for indoctrinating mass armies and waging 'total war'.

On the other hand nationalist doctrines are clearly not wholly responsible for the parlous state of international relations. Whatever Fichte, Renan and the sillier romantic dreams of nationalist propagandists in the nineteenth century may have claimed, most nationalist political leaders have shown realism in appreciating that the achievement of national political self-determination can neither eradicate all external dependence and obligations nor provide a universal elixir for world peace. When critics castigate nationalist doctrines for their aggressiveness and propensity for inducing political violence they are generally confusing nationalism in its *pure form* with doctrines of racial supremacy or ideologies of imperial aggrandisement. Given the conjunction of the rise of the nation-state with the collapse of absolute monarchy and the rise of republican democracy, was it not inevitable that the peoples of Europe should look to national identity and solidarity to provide a legitimation for their political autonomy? Were Gladstone, Asquith, Lloyd George (and Woodrow Wilson for that matter) so wrong to concede to Irishmen or Czechs or Poles the right to self-determination, freedom from an alien rule which their peoples had never endorsed or accepted? Surely it is natural justice that peoples who feel themselves part of a homogeneous national community should enjoy the dignity and status of national political autonomy, so long as it is admitted that such autonomy does not in itself resolve the pressing problems of internal political and economic justice, or the problem of creating a stable international order?

Major forms of nationalist movements

1 *Cultural-linguistic nationalism.* Many of the pioneers of Slav, Western European, Middle Eastern and African political nationalisms were *literati* who used their writings to project their consciousness of national distinctiveness and developed the initial claim for political independence. Nationalist leaders and intellectuals, once independence is achieved, may be displaced by other revolutionary political forces. Nevertheless, the newly independent nations, like their long-established ex-imperial rulers, rapidly appreciate the importance of cultural nationalism ('the battles of the books') for the intensification of their own peoples' national commitments.

In cases of long-standing imperial control or attempted elimination of political nationalism, cultural nationalism stubbornly survives. As the Soviet Union has found, it is almost impossible, in practice, to eliminate the linguistic identity and solidarity of an ethnic group. Indeed there is strong evidence, in Ireland and Wales in the nineteenth century for example, that the more the native language of an ethnic group is despised and deliberately discouraged by a government, the more it gains in mystique and significance as a secret language for the expression of their communal sufferings and hopes. Where the tradition of culture and language is still widely disseminated among an entire ethnic community it is entirely unrealistic, as was proved in the case of the Austro-Hungarian Empire in the nineteenth century, to hope to prevent a political phoenix arising from the embers of cultural nationalism simply by granting a limited imperial recognition of national cultural identity. Only when the larger proportion of an ethnic group has been assimilated into the politically dominant culture, as in modern Brittany or Wales,[25] does cultural nationalism survive as a doomed minority movement tragically unable to extend its cultural-linguistic base sufficiently to capture power by democratic means.

2 *Anti-colonial nationalism in the 'Third World'*. Nationalism was originally a European political doctrine, and it developed in the Third World as a by-product of colonial experience, accompanying or following the impact of colonial rule rather than preceding it. Herculean efforts at nation-building therefore proceed simultaneously with the construction of the political and administrative apparatus of a modern state. In most cases, however, it is by the accidents of colonial inheritance that the territorial configuration and the designated population, as well as the official language, educational system, and the major economic and administrative institutions have been determined. In such a setting, the appeals of doctrines of national self-determination to a European-educated but partially alienated and subordinated intelligentsia were absolutely overwhelming. Here, couched in terms that Europeans found immediately comprehensible, was the very rationalization they needed for their claims to run their own affairs, liberated from imperialist rule. To carry through their objectives, however, they had to create a national identity, consciousness and solidarity among their own people, a deep popular movement fired with a commitment to national independence. Not surprisingly, colonial governments at first attempted to crush such movements, though precise treatment varied according to the imperial power concerned and its political and military circumstances. A pragmatic colonialist tradition such as the British was

able to engender policies of actually encouraging or conniving with the new nationalists in the belief that the colonial power could thus more effectively weld the often disparate and warring tribes and religious communities into a stable and orderly polity.

The early colonial nationalists, however, very soon found themselves threatened by the outflanking economic revolutionism of socialist and Marxist movements. Those leaders who clung to a vague populist appeal, to an abstract millennialism, or to dependence on their charismatic predominance, have frequently paid the price for failing to deliver the material goods, a greater social and economic equality and improved living standards.

In many cases, especially in the British colonies, the colonial power's permissive rule encouraged the formation of nationalist parliamentary parties as a form of 'democratic tutelage', and where this happened the mass violence of a revolutionary overthrow of colonial rule was often avoided. In other circumstances, as in Cyprus, Algeria and Aden, nationalist movements found themselves suppressed or outlawed by the colonial government, and resorted to extra-legal, underground, guerrilla and resistance tactics in order to wrest control from their colonial rulers. Both revolutionary 'movements of national liberation' and essentially non-violent emergent nationalist parties require, above all, powerful bases of mass support and active participation if they are to wrest and hold power. The former type has to prove its popular legitimacy in the crucible of revolutionary war, and the latter has to prove its nationalist credentials to the departing power and to its own people. It should be stressed, however, that such movements may be far more ephemeral and unstable coalitions than has been hitherto assumed. Where such movements divide and collapse, the very possibility of a popularly legitimate regime, even the nascent sense of national identity and solidarity may be lost. In such a vacuum the way is open to determined minority groups, particularly the military officers with a monopoly of control over the coercive forces of the state, to snatch a *coup d'état*, rationalized as 'the maintenance of national unity' or 'preserving law and order'.

3 *'National conscience' and 'national rejuvenation'*. Mention of minority groups claiming to be guardians or saviours of 'national honour' or 'national unity' is a useful reminder that such parties and movements frequently arise in long-established nation-states. Normally they remain minority ultra-nationalist factions unless or until they ally with other groups on the authoritarian

right, such as monarchists, corporatists, Fascists and anti-Semites. By combining resources, as in Franco's National movement in the 1930s or in the Vichy coalition in France in the 1940s, they may then be able to take advantage of a period of national crisis, economic or political instability, or the shock of defeat in war, and seize political power.

Such movements are very close to Fascism but they are not identical with it. Those that are closest to Fascism, such as Charles Maurras' ultra-nationalist *Action Française*, tend inevitably to articulate more elaborate nationalist and quasi-racist doctrines and to appeal to a certain type of romantic literary intellectual. In the inter-war years they became almost indistinguishable from Fascism, though many stopped short of anti-Semitism of the pathological Nazi variety. Parties of 'national conscience' and 'national rejuvenation' claim to express and interpret the truest 'spirit of the nation', to be dedicated to the greatness and glory of the nation above all else. They pose as the 'praetorian guard' of national honour, constantly alert for the threat, not so much of external attack, but of betrayal or 'national subversion' from within. The true irony of their claim to be more royalist than the king is that their actions in what they consider to be the interest of national honour more often than not involve them in a mutiny or rebellion against the constitutional regime which they hold in such contempt. A classic instance of the *folie de grandeur* of military men and colonial and civil servants who are prone to pose as national saviours is that of 1958 when the lawful French government, faced with rebellion in Corsica and Algiers, was unable to depend on using its military aircraft to transport its security forces for fear that they would be flown in the wrong direction or be imprisoned by the rebels!

The events of 1958[26] showed another clear characteristic of 'national conscience' or 'national salvation' movements, that is, the constant mutual suspicion and in-fighting between the groups that comprise the movement coalition. In the Ruritanian situation of Algiers in May 1958, some of the plotters were working for de Gaulle's return to power without suspecting that the general might ultimately negotiate with the FLN, while others were plotting for an ultra-government without de Gaulle. Nevertheless, despite their often confused objectives and divided organizations, such movements constitute a very grave threat to parliamentary regimes in times of acute national strain such as colonial withdrawal or military defeat. The moral collapse of the Fourth Republic began at Dien Bien Phu to the extent that this defeat became the emotional catalyst for the movement to restore national honour.

One must conclude this brief review of forms of nationalist movement by stressing the importance and efficacy of the nationalist dimension as an additional source of legitimacy and as a propaganda instrument for national governments of any ideological persuasion. Churchill's appeals to the Britons' sense of duty in his war-time speeches, Harold Wilson's injunctions to stop 'selling Britain short' and Richard Nixon's posturing claim to be ensuring that America continues to be undefeated after her 'proud 190 year history' are all direct appeals to the popular nationalism. In the Soviet Union, Joseph Stalin's patriotic propaganda of the Great Fatherland War attempted to consolidate the nationalist base of 'socialism in one country' and national pride and national interest have been recurrent themes in Soviet foreign policy ever since. In practice, the author has not been able to find a single instance of a contemporary nation-state which has not found it as essential to draw on the capital of political nationalism as it has to use taxation and police powers.

Race movements

'Races' can be loosely defined as human groups sharing certain easily identifiable somatic characteristics, the most important of these being skin pigmentation. The historical processes of migration and miscegenation have brought about such enormous individual variations in colour of hair, eye colour, shape of skull, height and psychological characteristics that attempts to classify 'pure' racial types on the basis of such criteria are no longer scientifically practicable when applied to the overwhelming majority of the human species.[27] Colour, therefore, remains the universal badge of 'racial identity' in the popular mind, and provides both a signal and an excuse for racial prejudice, discrimination, persecution and conflict.

The wide occurrence of colour prejudice, however, is generally exacerbated by the dissemination of various racial myths which have been used to justify a particular 'pattern of dominance' or to provide quasi-ideological rationalization for the cruelest forms of racial persecution or the stirring up of race hatred. These racial myths may, however, base their concepts of 'racial identity' upon patterns of religious observance or kinship, or physiognomic characteristics, as was the case with Nazi anti-Semitism. Historical analyses of anti-Semitism have been attempted by Arendt and others.[28] In the present brief discussion, most of the illustrative examples have been drawn from the history of Negro emancipation, racial equality and racialist movements in America. The justification for doing so is that there is such a wide diversity of social movements involved in this history. Also, the classic literature covering most of these movements is readily available to the English-speaking student.[29]

1 *Racial emancipation and equality.* Indigenous racial emancipation movements arise in circumstances where a people subjected to slavery, peonage or other forms of domination, and possessing a sense of racial identity, seek to overthrow or to escape the existing structure of racial dominance. If the racially conscious group constitutes the overwhelming majority of the population within a state or colonial territory, the form of emancipation envisaged will normally be the removal of the dominant race from its position of political control. Such movements merge imperceptibly into Third World 'national' emancipation movements. If, however, the ethnic group remains a minority group exploited by an alien population and if the minority has been for several generations forcibly removed from the area of racial origin, then an agreed strategy of racial emancipation will inevitably be more difficult to find.

Should an oppressed racial minority be satisfied simply to attain a formal constitutional objective such as the abolition of slavery achieved by the abolitionists in the United States? How should the continuing economic exploitation of the minority (which long survives their emancipation from slavery) be most effectively resisted? A number of major alternatives present themselves. First they may, in the manner of the Jews under Moses, seek emancipation through migration to a 'promised land'. The territory normally conceived as the natural homeland is generally selected by criteria of religious myth, prophetic vision or historical tradition.[30] Unfortunately, the ethnic minorities may not be allowed, even after only a generation's absence, to return to their homeland. It may have been taken over by others. Racial emancipation movements, unlike some of the more ascetic religious sects, do not normally seek to create a homeland in one of the wildernesses of the world.

A second alternative is a struggle for racial separation, for the establishment of a territorial enclave to be wrested from, or conceded by, the dominant race. Such separation is normally envisaged as a 'nationalist' answer to the problem of an aggrieved ethnic minority. Within their newly defined territory the separatists envisage complete political, economic, cultural and religious autonomy for their race. Such appear to be the hopes of the US Negro Black Muslim movement, for example.[31]

Other racial minorities, especially those who constitute the remnants of the original pre-colonial population of a territory, may adopt bizarre millenarisms of the kind described in chapter 4, promising a supernatural intervention to turn the tables on their conquerors (for example the Bantu messianic cults and Melanesian cargo movements).

The fourth major strategy (the one most race relations experts and liberals of all races pin their hopes on) is that of peaceful assimilation into a multi-racial society on the basis of racial equality. This is the strategy of, for example, Malaya's race relations policy, the British Community Relations Commission, US civil rights legislation and the National Association for the Advancement of Coloured People.

Having identified the main alternative strategies of racial emancipation, the characteristics of the various movements involved must be briefly compared.

The actual struggle for the overthrow of slavery as an institution was necessarily grim and bitter. The slaves were placed at a pitiful disadvantage with no real prospect of freeing themselves without the intervention of external circumstances or division within the dominant race.

In the United States, for example, initially the Negroes were indentured, but as from the mid-seventeenth century they were being rapidly enslaved. By the mid-eighteenth century 2,500 slaves were imported, on average, annually. Between 1760 and 1770 the figure was 7,500. The reasons for this slavery, and for the evil 'triangular trade' which provided the human resources, were economic. It was more economical to keep plantation labour under slave conditions in perpetual servitude in days of acute labour shortage. Besides, Negro slaves, unlike white indentured labour, could easily be recaptured if they escaped the plantation.

The conditions in which slaves were kept have been compared by Stanley Elkins[32] to those of concentration camps. Rigid discipline, and the conditioning imposed by strict slave codes imported from the West Indies, combined to create a helpless, suffering passivity among the Negroes. It would be wrong to assume, however, that even the shocking inhumanities of slavery could quench Negro spirit or courage: their bravery and hope survived the crucible. Many daring groups such as that led by Nat Turner in the insurrection of 1831 attempted slave revolts. Nevertheless, they lacked opportunity and resources for organization, and the necessary weapons to defeat their masters. As was the case with the ending of slavery in the British Empire, the intervention of humanitarian, religious and political groups of whites opposed to slavery on moral or political grounds was ultimately decisive. Anglo-American humanitarian political and religious leaders combined to wage a powerful moral crusade between 1830 and 1861 against 'the peculiar institution'. Harriet Tubman, William Lloyd Garrison and Wendell Phillips were among their leaders.

Inevitably, Southern slave-owners who believed their economic survival depended on their right to keep Negroes as chattels, reacted by dressing up their pro-slavery arguments with quasi-religious arguments (see, for example, the Reverend Josiah Priest's *A Bible Defence of Slavery*, 1852) and assertions of presumed Negro biological and mental inferiority.

Whatever interpretation of the substantial causes of the American Civil War one may accept, the occurrence of the war and the eventual military defeat of the slave-owning South was, at least indirectly, the result of the enormous pressure built up by the abolitionist movement and the abolitionist wing of the Republican party, and the bitter conflict this engendered between North and South over the admission of new states to the Union.

Lincoln's reluctant and belated Emancipation Proclamation of 1863 and the Thirteenth Amendment to the Constitution in 1865 did not, however, end the economic exploitation of, and discrimination against, American Negroes. Nevertheless, many Negro-white coalition movements were henceforth encouraged to attempt the strategy of peaceful constitutional progress towards legal and economic equality. The achievements of these groups (such as General Otis Howard's Freedmen's Bureau, which distributed material and medical aid to Negroes, provided land for ex-slaves and helped Negroes get better jobs) have been largely unsung. Nevertheless, such early movements and later the National Association for the Advancement of Colored People (founded in 1910) did enormously valuable practical work for the betterment of Negro conditions. The special strength of the NAACP has been its effort, through the aid of Negro and white lawyers, to fight crucial court cases involving the enforcement of full civil rights for the Negro. These movements were prepared to work through the established social and political institutions, and to accept assistance from white or other racial groups whenever it was offered.

The strategy and tactics of such organizations as the National Urban League, which attempted to launch Negro housing programmes in the northern cities, and the NAACP, were essentially those of ethnic pressure groups. They lobbied legislatures and interviewed public officials from the president to small-town mayors; they gathered information of value to government agencies; and they co-operated in the framing of social policies. Rather than set up independent political parties, they lobbied members of both major parties and their own members often diverged in party identification within the broad spectrum of the coalition of Northern Democrats and liberal Republicans which developed on social issues.

By the 1950s there were signs that younger Negro leaders in the South, where anti-Negro discrimination and prejudice was virtually institutionalized, had become impatient with the pace and tactics, if not the strategy, of the 'gradualist' campaign for racial equality. Martin Luther King, who had been profoundly influenced by the teachings of Gandhi,[33] was the most influential exponent of techniques of moral protest, non-violent demonstration, freedom rides and 'sit-ins'. These tactics brought dramatic and effective publicity for the evils of racial discrimination and undoubtedly achieved real breaches in the Southern fortresses of institutionalized segregation. The tactics of King and the Southern Christian Leadership Council (SCLC) were novel in the context of US Negro movement and amazingly they produced rapid, tangible results (including the closing of arch-segregationist ranks behind openly racist leadership and brutal, often literally murderous, retaliation against civil rights workers). The rhetoric of the civil rights leadership became, under King's passionate and forceful personality, more inspiring and more urgent. He spoke of a revolution in values, of the need for a spiritual awakening which could bring about a genuine revolution in morality. This, he believed, could overcome the suspicion, hatred and fear that beset inter-racial relationships everywhere and bring about a relationship of loving and trusting fellowship. King was also convinced of the desperately urgent needs of the Negroes and the very poor of all races in America for essential material improvements in living conditions: better housing, education, job-training, employment opportunities and medical care. In short, he wanted a massive 'crash programme' of federally sponsored and funded social reform. In order to dramatize the urgency of the need for these provisions and to highlight the plight of the poor, King and the SCLC adopted the technique of a mass march of the poor, which had been pioneered by 'General' Coxey's Industrial Army fifty years earlier and by the unemployed in the great depression.

Of course it is true that the modern civil rights strategies and tactics are not entirely original in themselves. Why should they be? The problems and the obstacles that have to be overcome have endured for centuries. Progressives raged against the survival of Jim Crow laws in the South at the turn of the century. Socialists and populists alike have spoken passionately about the needs of the poor and the inhumanity of successive administrations' failures to provide for the welfare and future of the economically oppressed. It is not new for Christians to call for a revival of Christian values, nor to call on men to live in love and peace. What is important about King's contribution to the growth of the modern civil rights movement in America is precisely his ability to interrelate these concerns and commitments, to weld them into a programme. And through his passionate conviction and articulate style both as preacher and pamphleteer (see, for example, his magnificent, *Where Do We Go from Here: Chaos or Community*? 1967) he managed to persuade and galvanize into action not only Negroes of all classes, but many white liberals as well. Learning through the hard experience of confrontations with police, broken up demonstrations, infiltrations of his own *ad hoc* organizations by extremists, etc., King and his followers developed the civil rights movement by harnessing to their campaign for racial equality the tactics and organizational techniques of moral protest and non-violent resistance. Similar lessons have been learned and, tragically, forgotten, elsewhere.

2 *Racialism.* Leaders and followers within the essentially non-violent movements for racial equality are rapidly made aware of the pervasive and abiding appeal of racialist myths, not only among the hard core of their opponents striving for racial supremacy, but also among the masses. The generalized belief in the superiority of one's own race over all others, combined with a degree of popular xenophobia, is evinced in every period of history.

The attempt, however, to elaborate doctrines of racial supremacy in quasi-scientific terms is relatively recent (post 1800). A number of classic works have convincingly shown that such 'scientific' racial doctrines have absolutely no basis in biological or anthropological fact and it is not my purpose to review this debate here.[34] There is plenty of evidence, however, that racialist movements propagating and feeding upon these doctrines are still an active and enduring form of social movement. Juan Comas, in his well-known UNESCO pamphlet, *Racial Myths* (1958), has identified five extremely powerful racial myths all of which have been espoused by a wide variety of racialist movements: the myth of Negro inferiority; anti-Semitism and the myth of Jewish inferiority; the myth of the superiority of the 'pure', 'Aryan' or 'Nordic' races; the myth of the superiority of the 'true Anglo-Saxon'; and the myth of Celticism, or the innate superiority of people designated Celts. (Somewhat curiously, this notion is taken by some to include the majority of the French people!) One could add to this list the myth of Negro superiority and doctrines prescribing the achievement of racial supremacy by the Negro people.

There is no doubt that all these varieties of racialism gained a new lease of life from vulgarized versions of Social Darwinism and popular assumptions that the racial supremacy of the strongest nations of the world was in some way 'proved' by their relative success in the brute struggle for the survival of the fittest, a kind of natural selection of the 'highest' races. Furthermore, it is easy for intellectuals, who recognize the irrationality and historical confusions of racialist doctrines to underestimate the appeals of racialism to the uneducated and the very poor. In combating the prejudices and hatreds whipped up by racialism, one is confronting popular ignorance and fear of the 'unknown' stranger, a profound fear of economic competition for jobs, land, houses or resources, and an eagerness to accept the paranoid style of racialist movement which finds a 'racial conspiracy' an attractively simple explanation for all the world's problems.

In style of leadership and organization such movements tend to form a racialist conspiracy to counter the racialist conspiracy of their imaginations. They see everything in terms of 'them' and 'us'. To leave their movement is, in their eyes, racial betrayal. Racialist movements tend to be exclusivist, often adopting the passwords and disguises of the secret society (such as the Ku Klux Klan). Also, they often resort to conspiratorial and illegal acts. Para-military modes of organization and uniformed private armies are *par excellence* a feature of racialist movements (the classic example being Hitler's storm-troopers). This does not prevent them posing as parties of legality, fighting parliamentary elections, etc., when they scent a crisis that might bring them to political power. But when they are in a minority position, excluded from political power, they typically resort to hole-and-corner murders, thuggery, beatings-up and blackmail, and to intensive efforts to subvert youth by disseminating racialist doctrines among them. Though basically anti-Christian and anti-intellectual they are capable of infiltrating or manipulating these areas of social life for their own racialist ends.

Overt imperialism

The territorial aggrandisement sought by dynasties and peoples from remotest antiquity resulted from a tremendous variety of factors. Among them were: preservation of strategic advantage; the securing of a stable political order in conditions of anarchic conflict within and between states; material enrichment; missions of religious proselytization; the acquisition of a trading centre; and the enhancement of dynastic prestige. Such empire building can therefore be seen as the normal by-product of political and economic competition between dynasties and states. It did not have to be doctrinally justified to the mass of the population, because they, with only rare exceptions, did not share in the framing of foreign and defence policies. Such expansions of territory were assumed to be inescapable facts of world politics.

Even as late as the 1860s in Napoleon III's France the slogan 'imperialism' was taken to refer to the personal position of the emperor *vis-à-vis* the internal French political system rather than a programme of colonial expansion overseas. But between the 1870s and 1900 the modern doctrine of 'new imperialism', openly advocating and justifying colonial acquisition and the necessary military preparation for wars of colonial competition, had become a predominant obsession of powerful minority elements in the ruling classes and middle classes in all European states, and to some extent had taken root in the United States and Japan. This acceptance of 'overt' imperialism was intimately related to the hypertrophied nationalism of the period, pan-movements such as Pan-Slavism and various embryonic doctrines of racial supremacy.[35] Imperialist ideologies frequently elaborated the 'world mission' of an imperial power in great detail, defining its 'natural limits' and 'territorial entitlement' in the great power stakes. The ideological justifications that they provided leaned heavily on the vulgarized Social Darwinism, mentioned earlier, from which they drew the spurious conclusion that the 'natural selection' of the strongest empires or nations legitimated both their continued struggle for expansion and their 'beneficent' tutelage of 'inferior' peoples.

A distinction must be drawn, therefore, between the imperial expansion which resulted from the interplay of *historical movements or tendencies*—economic, military, political and cultural—and the overtly imperialist social movements such as the Imperial Federation League (founded 1884) and the Primrose League (founded 1883) in Britain, *Alldeutscher Verband* (the Pan-German League) in Germany, and the *Comité de l'Afrique Française* in France. Some of these organizations became, like the Primrose League, mass movements, while other more exclusive and informal groups such as Milner's 'Kindergarten' attempted to exercise pressure from within the political leadership.

Apart from their work as pressure groups, these imperialist movements were reinforced by sympathetic pro-imperialist elements within the military, the bureaucracy and the political parties. As the efforts of these movements were powerfully augmented by imperialist influences within the popular culture and through the early youth movements, their historical importance cannot be gauged by the size of their formal memberships alone. Nevertheless, the phase of the overt movements and leagues which frankly proclaimed the 'new imperialism' was relatively short-lived. Even by the 1930s in Britain the die-hard opposition of the Churchillian and the imperialist wing of the Conservative party to Indian Home Rule was widely considered an irrelevant and reactionary anachronism. It is true that, as in the case of French Algeria up to 1962, ultra-right colonialist factions were capable of rallying to uphold 'special cases' of imperial relationship. By the mid-twentieth century, however, few influential voices could be heard justifying territorial annexation and expansionism for its own sake. Imperialism, when it now occurs, is always of the 'covert' type, a by-product of economic exploitation or ideological conflict. 'Imperialism', drained of its original meaning, has become part of the normal vocabulary of political abuse, a slogan to be applied indiscriminately to all foreign policy actions to which exception is taken.

6/Reform and Moral Crusade

Normative interpretative problems

I have argued for the operational value of 'social movement' as a general type-concept in the study of social collectivities or groups. 'Social movement' was defined in chapter 1 as a deliberate collective endeavour to promote change, having at least a minimal degree of organization, and founded upon the normative commitment and active participation of followers or members. In chapters 3, 4 and 5, it has been proposed that a fairly comprehensive typology of social movement can be constructed, and that with the use of such a framework, it is profitable to examine some of the major concepts, theories and political implications of various major types of movement drawing on the extensive literature and using comparative analysis.

It has been shown that classification of social movements can be made relatively uncontroversially in the following ways: on the basis of their general field of concern (e.g. cultural, religious); according to their declared aims (e.g. racial equality, imperial expansion, colonial emancipation); or by using the criteria of their major constituency of popular support (e.g. labour, youth, women, peasants). Again it must be emphatically reiterated that even the use of these categories can be misleading, as few actual social movements conform precisely to an ideal type. Most combine the features of several movement types, have diverse goals and appeal to diverse constituencies of support.

However, it is when we come to analyse the most politicized movements, their ideologies, forms of political organization, strategies and political effects that we confront head-on the extremely important complications which originate from the fact that, as Heberle remarks, movements' strategies and organizations are interdependent with their ideologies. The difficulty is that movement interpretation has the inescapably normative character of any historical interpretation of human action.

On the one hand there are challenging, often daunting, empirical and methodological problems: identifying the political goals, principles or ideologies predominant in a given movement at a given time; deciding which leaders and ideas are in control; gauging the influence of oppositionist factions; recognizing changes in ideology, organization and strategy and evaluating their importance; identifying deliberate deception by leaders of movements and discovering what 'true intentions' may be camouflaged by propaganda. On the other hand there are the normative problems that arise from the human dilemmas of the contemporary historian or social scientist, who, in his personal and public life and actions as father, citizen or teacher, cannot avoid deciding where his own loyalties lie. Choice is forced upon him as upon us all. Shall he accept or reject the blandishments and appeals for support from movement *x*? To join or not to join? To resist or not to resist or to join in a strike? To accept conscription or resist the draft? To support or not to support a political party of whose policy he may approve only in part?

Except in the cases of acute schizophrenia or other forms of serious mental disturbance, it can be assumed that even the most determinedly objective scholar will be heavily influenced in his historical and analytical judgements by his own beliefs, experiences and modes of perception. For even the studied neutrality of 'objective social science' involves a *prise de position*, explicitly in the sense of a commitment to the ideals of scientific truth, scepticism and scientific freedom, and implicitly in that the doctrinal justifications and conversionist attempts of proselytizing ideological movements must have been rejected or withstood.

'Value-free' history or social science is not merely chimerical. Even if its attainment were possible it would be useless to mankind. Indeed, the intractable normative and prescriptive questions that have obsessed all serious political philosophers since the beginning of time, problems of ordering values and of the moral and political prerequisites of a better social organization or of a good society, have to be confronted openly in any useful discussion of the political implications of social movement. The methodological and empirical questions involved in obtaining accurate information about social movements and their development are nevertheless inextricably bound up with the philosophical questions which are of such long-term importance. How can one judge, or even begin to discuss responsibly, a movement's political ideology, its declared goals, or the moral and political desirability of its effects on its members, on other institutions or on international relations, unless one has adequate accurate factual information about the movement and its interrelations with other movements, society and polity?

While it is therefore very salutary to nail the myth of the 'value-neutral' social science,[1] this deflation neither necessitates nor excuses the abandonment of standards of liberal humane scholarship. The student of social movement has a dual obligation: both to serve historical truth and to provide carefully reasoned argument and evidence to support his judgements.

Organization and politicization

A drive towards movement politicization may find expression in a political ideology, in detailed policy proposals, as a protest in reaction against the policies of a regime or of other movements or institutions, or in the form of a declaration of dissent from one or more of a regime's legitimating values. But the political character of a movement's concerns and activities cannot be adequately understood or explained purely in political terms. The franchise reform movements in nineteenth-century Britain focused all their organizational energies upon the struggle for access to full rights of political participation and to a stake in political power through wider suffrage, but it would be wrong to assume that political power was sought for its own sake. Voting rights and ultimately the right to participate in or to support mass parties became recognized as the vital political *means* of obtaining wider economic and social opportunities and benefits, and of forcing the political and social élites to take action to avoid or mitigate the effects of economic disasters, depressions or wide-scale unemployment. Though not all protest movements and agitations necessarily arose directly from cyclical depressions, worsening economic conditions were certainly the most important single stimulus to working-class movement in nineteenth- and twentieth-century Britain.[2]

This generalization has very wide application in all cases of sudden and dramatic worsening of living standards, and of failures of material expectations, when hopes of betterment of conditions are suddenly dashed. When, however, economic depression and mass unemployment have a sustained and acute effect upon the working class the reverse of political movement may result, that is, apathy, introspection and a general atmosphere of hopelessness.[3]

Further, it should not be assumed that largely middle-class based reform movements remain totally unaffected by fluctuating economic conditions. Cobden had personal evidence of how a revival of trade aided the Anti-Corn Law League financially. In 1846 when the League was disbanded, a gift of £75,000 was made to him to compensate for the loss of his personal business, and the League as a whole was able to raise funds of '£50,000 in 1843 and about £90,000 in 1844'.[4]

However, some very interesting studies of middle-class radicalism have suggested that this syndrome results from the drive to express value-dissent, from the need for an outlet for moral protest. One argument put forward is that such expressions of moral opposition offer psychological satisfaction rather than any material benefits to participants and therefore such movements are unlikely to depend upon their participants' relative deprivation for their initial impetus.[5]

It is therefore hardly surprising that students of predominantly middle-class moral reform or protest movements find it profitable to explore the connections between religion and reform in order to ascertain the sources of value-dissensus and value-ambiguity. For, as Frank Parkin stresses in his study of the Campaign for Nuclear Disarmament (CND), those individuals most exposed to the exposition of spiritual values and ideals will become most sensitively aware of the disjunction between professed social ideals and social realities.

Therefore, Werner Sombart's aphorism, 'The foundations of the Social Movement is the social order to be attacked',[6] is an over-simplification, which arises from his exclusive concentration on proletarian movements. Furthermore, it is not completely accurate when applied to the Social Democratic movement in late nineteenth-century Germany with which Sombart is concerned. Both the initial stimuli to politicization, and the organizational forms and strategies adopted for political action vary according to circumstances of a movement's origin, the cultural, economic, political and religious conditions prevailing, and the 'social controls' or reactive devices resorted to by the political regime and major social institutions. The wide variations arising from differences of historical context and intellectual and political tradition should be borne in mind throughout the following brief discussion of major forms of political organization and strategy that have been developed or taken over by social movements.

There are several general problems concerning the organizational consequences of politicization which must be considered before recommencing our typological review. Firstly, there is the 'organizational paradox' which so many writers on organization and bureaucracy from Aristotle to Burnham and Michels have been aware of, that is, the tendency of mass movements to become institutionalized and bureaucratized in the very process of achieving political success or power. In fact, some may no longer be described as 'movements' for they can lose their commitment to change. The normative commitment and participation of members can atrophy either through a widespread disillusion or loss of zeal concerning the movement's aims, or as a direct consequence of the control of the movement organization by an oligarchic group manipulating a hierarchical bureaucratic structure of professional officials for its own power-seeking ends. But while it is easy to recognize examples of the tension and conflict between these two tendencies within given organizations—for example, between the more conservative, managerial, pragmatic party officials in the Chinese Communist Party (CCP) and the permanent revolutionism of the Red Guards—it is extremely difficult to determine when a movement has in fact reached the point of atrophy or elimination. In most large political organizations the movement dimension has a stubborn tendency to persist. Even where Michels' 'iron law of oligarchy' has long been in force, or where, as in the Communist party under Stalin, a revolutionary movement begins to devour its young, the movement symbols and legitimating values remain as potential rallying points for putative movement elements such as party dissidents, intellectuals or youth.

Secondly, attempts to link social movement with a specific form or phase of political organization or to establish the existence of general laws of movement development have been conspicuously unsuccessful. Jupp, for example, in his interesting monograph, *Political Parties* (1968), wishes to distinguish movements with 'their commitment to an ideology, their mobilization of enthusiasm, and their scorn for established political institutions and practices'[7] from political parties. Though he clearly envisages movements giving birth to parties he does not conceive of party-movement or movement-party phenomena. Jupp's definition of movement is, in any case, too confining: a clearly defined comprehensive ideology and scorn for existing political practices are not, as we have seen, essential prerequisites for social movement. Even those movements that have these characteristics, such as the Fascists, Nazis and Bolsheviks, have had frequent recourse to the 'party' label, and have entered parliamentary elections as a possible path to power. Radical 'mass parties', and labour movements such as the American and British trade union movements have retained movement organizations, methods of mobilization, and mass participation despite (or possibly because of?) their lack of ideological coherence. Such movements have been prepared to work for their goals within existing party structures, and have achieved considerable success from this strategy. While it is possible to make out a persuasive historical theory of movement 'deradicalization' or sectarian 'accommodation' in *certain historical instances*, as Tucker does for Soviet Marxism-Leninism[8] or Newton for the British Communist party,[9] we would be doing violence to history and deceiving ourselves by pretending that some *general scientific theory* of movement development or of the organizational consequences of movement politicization could be constructed on such bases.

Pluralism and mass society

Reformist agitations and pressure group campaigns do not involve the total rejection of societal values and norms: they are essentially concerned with minor or partial adjustments within an existing framework. Efforts may be directed at persuading the political élite that its policy or conduct of government ignores or undermines a basic value. Reformists may hold that specific policies or laws conflict with other more important values. Their claims that certain sections of a society are being adversely affected or victimized by certain policies may, on occasion, be accompanied by imputations of malicious intent on the part of political leaders. More generally, however, the good faith of the government is assumed, however slim the evidence in the government's favour, and reformers frame their grievances and demands in more measured terms in the hope of securing the tangible benefit of a measure of reform. Their classic strategy is to attempt to focus the attention of political leaders and the general public upon what they claim to be neglected social problems or issues, and upon the reformers' own proposals for dealing with such problems.

Clearly such movements can only operate freely and effectively in conditions of what can be broadly termed pluralist constitutional democracy. Essential among these preconditions are: a certain degree of tolerance of peaceful disagreement, criticism or dissent among political and social élites *and within the general population*; a wide dissemination of reliable factual information about policy proposals, existing policies, and policy effects among the political, social and economic élites which can be relayed to the general population through leaders of opinion and the mass media; the existence of a legislative forum and an identifiable executive upon which the reform movements and pressure groups have the acknowledged right to bring pressure to bear in the course of policy making, legislation and administration.

The continuity of such conditions is only guaranteed, furthermore, in certain circumstances. Firstly, the constitutional system must be preserved against attempted conquest from external or internal enemies; secondly, political control must not be seized by a putative dictatorship or totalitarian movement; and thirdly, reformist movements and pressure groups must be able to prove, by acquiring a record of effective campaigning, that the polity remains sufficiently flexible, energetic and resourceful, to adapt successfully to the necessities of changing conditions and demands. This last condition is given special prominence by theorists of pluralist democracy and by modern opponents of what are sometimes termed 'mass society' tendencies.

De Tocqueville, for example, in his *Democracy in America*, was one of the first to spell out a powerful argument for the indispensability of voluntary associations or organizations in a healthy, egalitarian and liberal democracy. Noting the tendency of Americans to 'constantly form associations' and to regard association 'as the only means they have of acting',[10] he asks whether there is 'in reality any necessary connection between the principle of association and that of equality'.[11] De Tocqueville concludes that there is such a vital connection. Associations perform the tasks of initiating ideas, advancing new projects, inventions and undertakings which a few wealthy powerful oligarchs are able to perform with ease in an aristocratic society. By contrast, citizens of a modern democracy (of which de Tocqueville takes the United States to be an ideal example) 'can hardly do anything by themselves, and none of them can oblige his fellow-men to lend him their assistance'.[12] Voluntary mutual assistance therefore becomes the vital means of preserving their independence from powerful individuals and from too much governmental intervention in their affairs. He concludes therefore in a well-known passage:

A government can no more be competent to keep alive and

to renew the circulation of opinions and feelings among a great people than to manage all the speculations of productive industry. No sooner does a government attempt to go beyond its political sphere and to enter upon this new track, than it exercises, even unintentionally, an insupportable tyranny; for a government can only dictate strict rules, the opinions which it favours are rigidly enforced, and it is never easy to discriminate between its advice and its commands.[13]

De Tocqueville, therefore, looks to strong voluntary associations to perform the functions of promoting fresh ideas and enterprises and preserving liberty, which had formerly been undertaken by wealthy aristocrats. Similarly, favourable pluralist views of the role of associational groups in democracy have been taken by theorists as diverse as Durkheim, Gierke, Maitland, Simmel, Figgis, G. D. H. Cole, Laski and Bernard Crick.[14]

An influential school of twentieth-century social theorists, from Karl Mannheim and Erich Fromm in the 1940s to Hannah Arendt and William Kornhauser in the 1950s,[15] has sought a partial explanation for the phenomena of the rise of totalitarianism in the decline or enfeeblement of secondary groups or associations, and in the rise of what is termed 'mass society'. These theorists contrast the 'mass society' in which all major social institutions are organized from the centre on a nation-wide basis (mass electorates, audiences, markets, etc.) with the concept of the traditionally segmented village-centred life and relationships of rural communities. Kornhauser (1968) proceeds from the assumptions that city dwellers often experience 'isolation' and 'anomie' and 'anonymity' and that their religious, ethnic and social class ties gradually weaken as sources of distinctive values, coherence, uniqueness and influence. He argues that city dwellers show increasing uniformity of outlook and are influenced by mass organizations of a more formal, bureaucratized and egalitarian type, which become the 'characteristic units' of mass society.

The 'mass society' theorists argue that the pressures of mass organization and mass egalitarianism lead to the worship of numerical superiority as the measure of success, to constant competition for mass popularity, and to attempts at mass manipulation, mobilization and control.

Kornhauser derives a theory of mass movements from mass

society theory. Within a developing mass society, he argues, the population will tend to dichotomize into those who have already been assimilated into mass relations and organizations, and groups which remain locally attached: i.e. between new and old classes. Thus 'the locally attached, in their resentment of ascendancy of big cities, big government, big business and big labour, become receptive to the appeals of mass movements directed against the forces of mass society'.[16] These groups are joined, asserts Kornhauser, by those newly mobile groups who have left rural communal relations but who still remain unassimilated into mass society—for example, new factory workers, and new migrants to cities. Such people are more 'readily available for activistic modes of intervention in political life and participation in mass movements that promise them full membership in the national society'.[17] Such mass movements attempt to create entirely new and direct links between mass movement leaders and followers rather than to 'build on existing social relations'.[18]

In *The Politics of Mass Society* (1959), Kornhauser's analysis of mass society theory concludes that democratic societies are especially vulnerable to penetration and control by totalitarian movements when they lack strong secondary organizations or associational groups capable of 'mediating' between élites and non-élites. Mass movements, according to his theory, are most likely to occur among social classes who have suffered the trauma of acute social crisis (e.g. war or mass unemployment), and will especially appeal to those with the fewest social ties, such as freelance intellectuals, small farmers and small businessmen. He therefore endorses de Tocqueville's argument that where social pluralism is strong, liberty and democracy will be strong.

Another recent study by Lipset, Trow and Coleman (1956) similarly argues that 'democratic politics necessarily rests on a multitude of independent organizations, the manifest functions of which need not be political'.[19] This study anticipates Kornhauser's own checklist of the major functions of such associations: they act as sources of new ideas, as channels of communication, as media of political education and for training in skills of self-government and political opposition, as a means of widening political participation, and as bases of opposition to the central government. Like Kornhauser, Lipset *et al.* stress that pluralist groups can only be made powerful enough to resist the monopolist tendencies of élites if they have sources of power which are truly independent of the government and provided that political élites are constitutionally and effectively constrained to compete for political leadership.

This influential school for modern pluralists persuasively augments the classic case for the interdependence of association and liberty. The 'mass society' hypothesis usefully focuses our attention upon the socio-psychological consequences of mass urbanization, mass organization and bureaucratization in industrialized societies. Yet, I would argue, its developmental theory of social change is narrowly deterministic and essentially inadequate. Mass society tendencies are invoked as the most significant, if not comprehensive, explanation for the rise of totalitarian movements. But mass society theorists do not begin to explain why some highly industrialized societies have developed powerful totalitarian movements while others have not. No adequate empirical evidence has yet been adduced to prove that, in certain societies, populations are foredoomed to a state of nihilism, apathy or 'privatized' docility. Furthermore, how is one to identify a quantitative increase in 'social alienation' (which Kornhauser defines as the 'distance between the individual and his society')? Again, although a totalitarian movement or regime will, by definition, attempt to bring all secondary group activity under its own central control, we have no evidence for assuming that pluralist groups in non-totalitarian societies have entered on a period of inevitable decline.

The crudest and most spurious feature of mass society theory is its vague and indiscriminate use of the concept of 'social alienation'. Complete social alienation is inconceivable outside a psychiatric ward. As Frank Parkin observes in his study *Middle-Class Radicalism* (1968), *partial* rather than complete alienation from societal values and norms is a widespread and not surprising phenomenon. When this occurs it is quite probable that such partial value alienation will be experienced by those who are already most aware of, and highly committed to, other values which they regard as of greater importance or by those who are acutely aware of evaluative ambiguities, claiming that the political élite or their opponents have misunderstood a specific value. Furthermore, as Parkin discovered in the cases of the CND supporters he studied, it can be shown that persons who give expression to value dissent in the form of radical movements, far from being bereft of social ties or group involvements, show abnormally high participation in secondary organizations (churches, educational and recreational associations, etc.). A degree of alienation from societal values can, therefore, be positively correlated to a high rate of involvement in group life, and it may act as a catalyst for further associational promotion and participation. Moreover, new forms of secondary organization need not necessarily be limited to totalitarian or mass political organizations.

This brings us to another grave weakness of mass society theory, which is its failure to describe or explain the rise of the pluralist associations and groups whose existence it claims to be so vital to the survival of democracy.

Reform agitations

Let us consider the exponential rise of extra-parliamentary reform agitations and associational and promotional groups in the early and mid-nineteenth century. It is true that this was a period when the 'mass society' tendencies of urbanization, industrialization and bureaucratization were operating with dramatic intensity in British society. But these general historical trends, however weighty their consequences, do not in themselves provide adequate explanation for the proliferation of reformist agitations. The specific social movements involved arose from a diverse array of often overlapping and interconnected commitments to change the existing social and political institutions. The major pressures were: the drive to challenge the predominance of the landed interest over the political and socio-economic élites; the rise of the *nouveaux riches*, the new middle classes of businessmen and manufacturers who demanded a say in government; the movement to overturn or severely modify the political and religious settlement of 1688; the drives of non-conformists and Catholics for equality of civic rights and socio-economic status with their Anglican brethren; and the movement to curtail or reduce mercantilist government intervention in economic affairs.

Nor can one satisfactorily explain or understand the movements which expressed these commitments simply in terms of their relation to changing economic and material interests or as mere reflections of class interest. In fact, many of these movements were themselves direct outgrowths of religious and intellectual movements such as the Quaker-Evangelical humanitarian reform coalition. They also drew upon the traditional radicalism of the mid- and late-eighteenth century (Fox, Wilkes, Tom Paine, Julian Harney), on French Revolutionary ideas, and from the newly asserted Benthamite emphasis on maximizing hedonist utility as a guiding principle of reform.

The early nineteenth-century reformist agitations were often multi-dimensional (i.e. they very often had diverse or conflicting aims) and they generally overlapped in membership and aims with many other groups. Thus it was not unlikely that an active reformer could be a participant in the early trade union movement, the Chartists and the factory movement, at the same period. Many humanitarian movements such as anti-slavery and penal reform societies were very often, if not exclusively, outgrowths or sub-movements of larger and more amorphous religious movements.[20]

The reformist agitations of nineteenth-century Britain were very often campaigning on behalf of classes or sections of society excluded from the governing élite and denied full civic rights, for example, the successive franchise reform movements, and the factory movement. But most of the financial contributions, the leadership and the organizational expertise was provided inevitably by middle-class activists who were committed to initiating or amending legislation. Most of these reform movements wound up when the statutory victory had been won although some more enduring associations remained as semi-permanent pressure groups on behalf of various specialized reform interests, e.g. the Anti-Slavery Society, the Howard League for Penal Reform and the Health of Towns Association. In many cases the setting up of new machinery of central and local government was seen to be the most lastingly effective consequence of reform and the need for 'watch-dog' pressure group activity by private associations was not, therefore, found to be so compelling after its establishment.

By comparison, ideologically amorphous and largely working-class based movements such as the Chartists[21] could claim less immediate success. Their reform programme was at once too sweeping, radical and ambitious to become practical politics. The fissiparous character of their movement, divided as it was between moderates, socialists and 'physical force' factions, was also an insuperable handicap. Nevertheless, much of the radical political reformism of the Chartists and their organizational experience later became harnessed to the more enduring organizational forms of working-class movement—the trade unions, co-operative societies and the embryo socialist parties.

Pressure group campaigns

Some pressure groups never seek or acquire a mass membership. For example, employers' confederations, special industrial lobbies, and *ad hoc* groups of 'interests' or 'experts' frequently operate as small private cliques or informal groups within the political, social or economic élites, in an endeavour to influence policy-making without any resort to press or TV campaigns, mass rallies, public meetings or demonstrations of any kind. Other pressure groups have mass membership and movement dimension from their inception, while some movements develop pressure group organizations and strategies at a later stage in their history, as was the case with the trade union movement. The defining characteristic of such pressure group organizations is that group leaders and members are already integrated into full participation in the political system and such groups have full and recognized rights of access to executive and legislative organs of government.

Pressure groups may adopt strategies of departmental consultation and submission of reports and evidence to government committees, and also strategies of propaganda, 'public education' or mass lobbying or demonstration to win support and to show their solidarity and determination. Whichever strategy is adopted, however, the movement dimension of pressure groups with a mass membership can prove both a boon and an embarrassment to their leaderships.

The major advantages of an expanding mass membership are cumulative and are therefore of greatest value to the largest, most bureaucratized and professionalized pressure groups. It ensures, for example, the financial future of the group by providing an ever-increasing income from subscriptions. Moreover, if the group secures either a monopoly or a clear predominance over the eligible constituency of the sectional interest concerned (as is the case with the National Farmers' Union or the Association of University Teachers) the group's prestige and status is enhanced. In addition, where the group's leaders or negotiators wish to use the threat of sanctions as a bargaining counter, the size of the mass membership who could withhold their services, labour, electoral votes, etc., may be the determining factor in the conflict of interests. Also, for the techniques of mass lobbying and demonstration, a sizeable and committed movement following is a vital prerequisite.

A further advantage is that, in a pluralist system with wide and frequently overlapping group memberships, a group's stock of information and policy proposals can be vastly enriched by the participation of a membership of diverse talents and experiences. For example, the early work of the municipal public health reform movement was vitally dependent on the scientific information and expert schemes put forward by Medical Officers of Health and high ranking administrators, albeit acting in a private capacity. Similarly, church pressure groups such as the British Council of Churches have been able to call on the valuable expertise of laymen who are specialists in other professions for the purpose of guiding the council, or of assembling or evaluating evidence for the churches. Most groups with an active mass membership also gain greater solidarity and higher intensity of commitment by maintaining democratic processes of election and policy making within their own organizations.

Obvious disadvantages of the movement dimension are felt by some groups: there may be bitter internal wrangles or splits among the mass membership or between members and leaders (a problem not unknown in the BMA and NFU as well as the industrial trade unions!) which may severely damage the group's unity, credibility and capacity for action.

One feature that should be stressed in this brief characterization is that, outside the mass of trade unions which are specifically working-class movements, most voluntary associations or pressure groups with a movement dimension have a predominantly middle-class membership and leadership. Both the voluntary association and the pressure group are *par excellence* agencies of middle-class mobilization and influence.

A final footnote should be added to this brief comment on the movement dimension of pressure groups. There is a serious dearth of published research dealing with grass-roots organizations, structures and processes of pressure groups with mass memberships.[22] And until such time as this is rectified a disjunction between social movement theory and pressure group theory is likely to remain, to their mutual detriment.

Moral crusade and moral protest

Although some of the more frenetic and confused student protest movements of the late 1960s frequently sought to give the impression that they personally invented morality, moral crusade and moral protest form an important traditional element of social movement. Moral conviction, passion and a sense of moral outrage do not appear to be the monopoly of any civilization, period, social class or age group. Populist and reformist movements, in particular, have displayed a high moral zeal and have frequently indulged in moral condemnation of their opponents and in quasi-religious techniques of propaganda and conversion. They have made extensive use of religious doctrines, symbols, hymns and prayers as well as the sermonizing public lecture and inspiratory calls to battle. Their most salient characteristics are their religious or quasi-religious appeals to faith in absolutes, and the kind of intensity of faith or depth of commitment which inspires enormous courage, heroic self-sacrifice and even martyrdom, for their causes.

Another important feature which such movements have long had in common with religious movements, at least since the religious wars of the seventeenth century, is a tendency to eschew premeditated strategies of public violence. They see physical violence as fundamentally immoral and therefore to be avoided lest their actions should be seen to contradict their own claim to rectitude. By 'bearing witness', even 'carrying the cross' of persecution, they intend that the moral truth they proclaim will win out. They strive to win the moral victory in the long run even if it cannot be finally achieved until 'judgement day'.

This is not to suggest, of course, that moral crusaders and protesters are always able to avoid conflicts with counter-movements or security forces. The point is that for moral crusade movements it is a *sine qua non* that deliberate physical force strategies should be rejected. Moral victories can be won in the hearts and minds of both opponents and indifferent bystanders only by superior moral persuasion, by making evident the superiority of the movement's version of the truth. Indeed, as Martin Luther King argued in connection with the Negro civil rights campaign, to resort to violence will lead in all probability to an escalation of the moral evil which is being attacked: 'In the guilt and confusion confronting our society violence only adds to the chaos. It deepens the brutality of the oppressor and increases the bitterness of the oppressed . . . It destroys community and makes brotherhood impossible.'[23]

A further characteristic of the moral crusade and protest *sui generis*, especially in its contemporary form, is its ideological amorphousness and ambiguity. These movements are concerned above all with great issues: the averting of nuclear war, the ending of war in Vietnam, ending schools segregation in the US, opposing apartheid and so on. Beyond these commitments to generalized aims there is no common ideological consensus within the movements, either on the means by which such aims are to be realized, or upon a general programme of social and political reforms. In the case of the moral protest movements it is easier to tell what they are 'against' than what they are 'for'. Moral crusades and protests tend, therefore, to be heterogeneous issue coalitions, enabling many groups, frequently in bitter rivalry with each other on other issues and on general principles, to combine temporarily under a specific campaign's organizational umbrella.

Moral crusade and protest are not usually generated by selfish desires for material benefits on the part of the participants. But this does not mean, as Blau argues,[24] that their conduct must necessarily be dismissed as irrational. Their collective action is directed towards asserting, redefining or defending ultimate moral values. Frank Parkin in *Middle Class Radicalism*, a study of the CND, very effectively deploys Blau's concept of 'expressive' politics to convey the particular functions and style of the morally assertive movement. The satisfactions and 'rewards' to be gained through such movements are seen to be primarily, if not exclusively, emotional and psychological: they spring from what Weber terms the 'ethic of ultimate ends' rather than the 'ethic of responsibility'.[25] Parkin is surely correct to stress 'the fact that individuals may support political movements because they symbolize the rejection of, or identification with, certain values . . .'[26]

Who supports, or participates in, such movements? Parkin has some useful evidence and clarification about the social bases of the CND which, he argues forcefully, may provide an explanatory theory generally applicable to *middle-class* radicalism. It is worth stressing this deliberate emphasis of Parkin's work at the outset, because clearly it would be false to assume that moral awareness, crusade and protest are purely middle-class phenomena. The radicalism of the working classes has never been exclusively concerned with bread and butter causes. Such a narrow hedonism would not, in any case, be rational in a human situation in which *the whole society* is affected by the long-term value orientations and authoritative allocations of political decision-makers. (Had British working-class protest and action against the cotton-growing Confederates in the US Civil War no moral dimension? Should we assume that working-class action to prevent allied intervention against Bolshevism, and the later opposition to Franco's Fascism and Nazi persecution of the Jews in the 1930s were solely motivated by material class interest?) There is abundant evidence of moral commitment among working-class radicals, and of the crucial role of working-class intellectuals and leaders in all the great radical crusades.[27] But militant, 'morally committed' working-class radicals are clearly a small minority of their class, just as middle-class radical activists are of theirs.

The important questions about membership and support of moral crusade and protest movements are concerned with the problems of identifying the social, religious, educational and occupational backgrounds of the radical minority within a total population. Parkin, for example, attempts to grapple with these problems in his study of the CND. He finds the CND to have been overwhelmingly middle-class supported, with 83 per cent of his sample respondents drawn from professional, managerial and white-collar worker groups.[28] The question is: From which sections of the middle class were they drawn? He finds that 54 per cent of his sample had received some form of higher education and that the heaviest occupational concentrations of CND supporters appeared in the 'welfare' and 'creative' professions rather than within the wide range of commercial and managerial posts. Parkin assesses the alternative explanations put forward for the widely observed correlation (which he had confirmed in his own study) between such occupations as social work, teaching and librarianship, and involvement in radical politics.[29] Though he sensibly refrains from dogmatically imposing any single explanation, he does suggest that his researches provide some support for Gerhard Lenski's theory of status crystallization.

Lenski argues[30] that persons whose various statuses (ethnic, occupational, economic, etc.) are out of congruence with one another will be more likely to support left-wing attitudes than persons whose statuses are approximately congruent. Parkin suggests that the combination of very low economic status and high professional status of the typical, poorly paid CND welfare worker or teacher may, therefore, provide a partial explanation of the radicalism of these CND supporters.

Parkin clearly distinguishes certain important sub-groups of CND supporters. First, there was a radical Christian minority for whom the 'Sermon on the Mount is considered to be not simply a doctrine of personal goodness but a charter of government and international relations as well'.[31] This group tended to see the CND as a means of implementing the social gospel of Christianity, as a means of rejuvenating the established churches and restoring their moral influence, and 'as a model of what the church itself should be'.[32] Parkin concludes: 'Christian protest against the Bomb and support for CND has therefore symbolized protest against the organized church and its ministry, and the dialogue concerning nuclear weapons has also been a dialogue on the role of religious witness in contemporary Britain.'[33]

The mass society theorists and psycho-pathologists of social movement have tended to single out the intellectuals as being the group very largely responsible for inspiring and promoting mass movements and for providing them with symbols and powerful appeals. Parkin quite correctly rejects these unhistorical and sweeping generalizations and distinguishes a group of 'socially unattached intelligentsia' from the majority of intellectuals. He derives the term 'socially unattached intelligentsia' from Karl Mannheim in order to denote those freelance creative intellectuals (novelists, dramatists, painters, poets and freelance designers, for example), who do not have privileged, secure, institutional bases in society and who are at the mercy of the cold commercialism of market pressures. By contrast, Parkin notes, the majority of British intellectuals have been relatively conformist and secure, supported by university posts, the BBC, the British Council and publishing houses, on relatively comfortable salaries and pension schemes. The price that the institutionalized intellectuals pay for their relative security is the acceptance of bureaucratic constraints on their freedom to voice radical dissent and to indulge in radical protest organization. As might be expected, it is the 'socially unattached intelligentsia' who are found to have provided the bulk of intellectual energy and passion for the CND. Such figures as Bertrand Russell, Kingsley Martin, Marghanita Laski, J. B. Priestley, John Arden and Vanessa Redgrave fall into this category.

Parkin argues that, as in the case of the radical Christian minority of supporters, the intellectuals involved were engaged primarily in a form of symbolic protest: 'protest against the Bomb was often a thinly-veiled protest at certain other aspects of the social order which were independent of the Bomb, but which the latter appeared dramatically to highlight'.[34] In the case of the freelance intellectuals, for example, Parkin makes out a very convincing case that the post-war generation of artists (especially the dramatists who were so active in the CND) 'were radicalized largely as a result of the sharp discontents they experienced in attempting to introduce new cultural standards into a traditional setting dominated by a commercial ethic . . .'[35]

Analysing youth participation in the CND, Parkin's findings endorse those of S. M. Lipset[36] and many others concerning student radical movements, to the effect that only a small minority of middle-class youth is involved in such action. The 'political generation' hypothesis that each successive generation's philosophy and political attitudes are entirely remoulded by their common historical experiences is firmly rejected. The evidence of recent studies in the UK[37] suggests that youth's politics are basically conformist, despite the constant recurrence of international crisis and the threat of nuclear war. Youth as a whole tends to reflect the political attitudes of its parents. The problem for students of moral protest and crusade movements is to identify and to attempt to account for the youth minority (or what Mannheim calls 'generation-unit') which is radically engaged.

Parkin deploys the most compelling evidence in favour of the theory that the most decisive influence directing youth into radical movement is family socialization. No less than 62 per cent of Parkin's CND respondents claimed that at least one parent approved of or supported the CND, and the 'great majority of respondents' came from homes 'where there is some level of commitment to left-wing politics on the part of both parents'.[38] Parkin also stresses the youthful appeals of marching and demonstration activity, of the excitement and self-sacrifice involved and of the 'good fellowship' of the movement.

Modern moral crusade and moral protest movements are confronted with extremely testing problems of political strategy. To add to their traditional repertoire of public meetings, processions, marches, demonstrations, the presentation of petitions, mass lobbying of legislators and pamphleteering, moral crusades have developed new means for exerting moral and psychological pressure—planned mass civil disobedience, 'sit-ins' and 'freedom-rides'. Many of these are consciously borrowed from earlier movements: for example, Martin Luther King and student civil rights leaders took over some of the strategies of civil disobedience that Gandhi had developed to such good effect. The controlled use of such strategies can be most impressive and morally persuasive, but there are serious risks involved. If the 'marshals' or leaders lose control of the demonstration, there is always the danger of open conflict with the police or the military, or counter-demonstrations and a subsequent escalation of violence that will only serve to damage the cause. Furthermore, there is a risk, spelt out by the conservative majority opinion of the US National Commission on the Causes and Prevention of Violence,[39] that successive acts of civil disobedience will tend to bring the law into contempt and weaken the judicial authority upon which the security of the whole society, including the demonstrators, depends.

The strategy of civil disobedience also depends for its chance of success upon a fine calculation of the intentions and coercive potential of the governmental authorities. In a relatively law-abiding democratic society in which the political leadership is exceedingly reluctant to resort to armed force to suppress demonstration, resourceful and determined civil disobedience can have considerable short-term success in baulking the will of the authorities. This was the case, for example, when the British Ministry of Defence was successfully prevented from using the Pembrey range in Carmarthenshire, Wales, in November 1969, by a determined movement of local opponents. Mass civil disobedience in a situation of international or internal war, on the other hand, could be purely suicidal. Military commanders unleashing their forces in mortal combat are unlikely to allow themselves to be checked, or their tactical or strategic advantage to be put at risk at the hands of morally committed but unarmed civilians. On the crucial question of whether non-violence can force a conqueror to withdraw, one's judgement must be reserved.[40] Certainly there is no clear-cut historical evidence to date that it can do this, and it is therefore highly likely that the effective use of civil disobedience as a strategy of moral crusade and protest will be confined to the domestic politics of pluralist regimes.

For all moral crusade and protest movements, however, whether they employ traditional strategies or newer approaches of planned civil disobedience, the criterion of success is their long-term influence in remoulding public opinion concerning the moral issues that inspire them. A very determined, broad-based moral issue coalition can show political returns over a relatively short period. In this context, one could cite the effect of the 'no more war' and 'peace pledge' movements of the 1920s and 1930s and the psychological constraints their pacifism imposed upon the foreign and defence policies of inter-war governments. A further example is the cumulative influence of the anti-Vietnam War campaigns and the 1969 Vietnam moratorium upon the shaping of American policy in Vietnam and the policy of phased withdrawal of US troops. Again, in the long term, moral crusades can help to induce the members of the political élite, if not the general population, to abandon long-held customs such as judicial flogging and capital punishment.

Historically, moral crusade and protest has, like religious movement, often proved its capacity to transcend national frontiers. For example, the movement for abolition of slavery became a trans-Atlantic movement, and the great peace movements of the 1930s, such as the International Peace Campaign organized in League of Nations countries, were often organized on a genuinely international basis, operating as international pressure groups and proselytizing movements. These are examples of the many distinguished precursors of the international anti-nuclear weapon, conservationist and anti-Vietnam War movements of the late 1960s.

A further point I wish to note about moral crusade and protest is its relationship to putative totalitarian movements. As we shall have reason to note when we consider revolutionary movements, it is a frequent tactic of totalitarian movements to join protests and to exploit them for their own purposes. This tactic is by no means always successful. If a moral crusade has been inspired and promoted by other groups and these initiators succeed in sustaining a high level of idealism and moral commitment to the organization, it is almost impossible for one minority in the coalition to impose its will and ideology upon all the other participants. There will not be, in these circumstances, sufficient apathy or ignorance among the membership to enable a totalitarian group to capture key organizational posts. Under these circumstances, the totalitarian ideologues have to content themselves with simply associating their group with the public demonstrations of the moral crusade and using the opportunity of personal contacts in the movement to publicize their own ideas and possibly to recruit new members.[41]

7/Class and Revolution

Working-class action and mass parties

Who are the working classes? Ever since the origins of permanent human settlement there must have been classes of serfs, peasants, servants, labourers, all performing the vital work of menial labour as the 'pack-horses' of society. Many of them, particularly at periods of unbearable exploitation, participated in the early millenarisms, urban riots and populist revolts discussed in previous chapters. Marx, who took over the conception of socio-economic class from the Scottish Philosophical Radicals and the historians of the French Revolution, extended his own theory of class to embrace pre-industrial societies. Nevertheless, as we have noted, Marx's major preoccupation was with the class relations that resulted from the new means of production developed in the course of the industrial revolution. More narrowly still, the intense interest of both historians and contemporaries in the birth of the factory system has led to an identification of the masses of factory hands as the 'new working class'. Precisely because England pioneered industrial revolution it was the English working population which first experienced class identification, class consciousness, class antagonism and class action in this modern sense. Inevitably, in the dramatic setting of English industrialization, British economic theorists of society rapidly developed analytic concepts of class. We have already noted that Marx, in the course of developing his theories, was extensively influenced by this whole literature and intellectual and popular debate that accompanied it, as well as by the findings of parliamentary reports and inquiries and such contributions as Engels' *The Condition of the Working Class in England* (1844). It is to the important, relatively recently enriched, literature on the rise of class and class action in England that I shall turn to introduce a brief discussion on movements of working-class action.

Professor Harold Perkin in his work, *The Origins of Modern English Society 1780–1880* (1969), contrasts the class society which he sees developing in the early decades of the nineteenth century with what he terms 'the Old Society' of the eighteenth century. This society was 'first of all an aristocracy, a hierarchical society in which men took their places in an accepted order of precedence, a pyramid stretching down from a tiny minority of the rich and powerful through ever larger and wider layers of lesser wealth and power to the great mass of the poor and powerless'.[1]

Professor Perkin provides an extremely convincing explanation for the fact that the class feeling and antagonism latent in late eighteenth-century England did not succeed in finding full, overt expression until the 1810s and 1820s. The key to the problem lies in the interdependence of the rise of working-class consciousness and the development of working-class industrial and political movement. In common with E. P. Thompson, E. Hobsbawm and many other modern historians of the period, Professor Perkin accepts that many outbursts of machine breaking and destructive rebellion in the eighteenth century can be explained as manifestations of class antagonism, and that workers' resentment of the higher orders was often 'diverted into religion'.[2] But what was required to transform these elemental and sublimated forms of class resentment into that fully-fledged working-class consciousness which E. P. Thompson has defined as, 'the consciousness of an identity of interests as between all these diverse groups (out-workers, domestic workers, factory hands, etc.) of working people and as against the interests of other classes'?[3]

Professor Perkin maintains: 'The explanation lies in the total social situation of the individual. Of this, source of income and the vertical antagonism it generates are but a part, and, though important, can operate freely and effectively only in large-scale communities, where the individual can unite with many others of his kind to defeat the ubiquitous pressures of personal dependency.'[4] This quotation succinctly illuminates the decisive role of working-class political and industrial movements in the formation of working-class consciousness and the rise of working-class political influence.

I do not intend to dwell on the interesting subject of the development of multiform working-class economic organizations and mutual-help associations, trade unions, co-operatives, friendly societies and so on. The interested student is referred to the many scholarly histories and analyses of these organizations.[5] The intention here is to review briefly the major political strategies and organizations developed specifically by and for the working class as movements for class action, and in their self-perceived class interests.

Whatever the form of political organization and strategy adopted at any given time, all working-class movements have not only actively helped to decide the shape of social and political institutions and societal values and norms, but have also been to some extent moulded and influenced by what Professor Perkin terms 'the social consequences of industrialism'. The exponential increase in the scale of urban conglomeration in the period of nineteenth-century industrialization magnified the effects of slumps and cyclical unemployment. Perkin observes:

> In the first half of the nineteenth century every major slump produced its wave of political protest, every major political crisis coincided with a period of marked distress. The post-war depression of 1815–20 triggered off the first mass movement for Parliamentary Reform. The Reform crisis of 1830–32 coincided with the downswing of a major depression. The birth, climax, and dying throes of Chartism in 1837, 1842 and 1848 all occurred in the troughs of slumps, the climax in the worst depression of the nineteenth century.[6]

It would be quite wrong to assume, however, that there is any simple cause and effect relationship between severe social distress and alignment to radical politics. Indeed, as has been noted earlier, right up to the end of the eighteenth century the alliance of landowning aristocracy and the urban mob behind the monarchy and traditional aristocratic government, the so-called 'church-and-king' mob, was a far more common phenomenon than radical working-class politics.[7] Moreover, if we look at what are often taken to be the first radical working-class organizations proper in England—the Corresponding Societies of Sheffield, Derby, Manchester and London, founded in the late eighteenth century—we discover that their radicalism was by no means a direct consequence of the rise of the new factory system. It was a continuation and refinement of the old dissenting radical tradition which had existed in England since the Levellers.

The London Corresponding Society founded in 1792, with the artisan Thomas Hardy as secretary, certainly reflected in its ideas and debates the more cosmopolitan radicalisms and the heterogeneous occupational links of its members. E. P. Thompson has suggested[8] that, nevertheless, the London Society had certain features that marked it out as a prototype working-class movement: a low weekly subscription, the purely social as well as political and economic interests of the organization, and a working-class secretary. Most important of all, in Thompson's view, is the first rule of the society—'that the number of our Members be unlimited'—for this highlighted the society's aims of mass proselytization and mass mobilization.

These defining characteristics of working-class political movement recur constantly through the great reform battles of the early nineteenth century; in the rise of the Owenite Movement, in the Ten Hours movement, during the 1831–32 crisis, and in the Chartist phenomena. Their political strategies were diverse, pragmatic and frequently unsuccessful. Working-class organizations initiated, or lent support to, a whole host of reformist agitations, strikes and industrial actions: for franchise reform, against child labour in factories and mines, for a ten-hour working day, against truck shops, against wage reductions, for wage increases, for the right to join unions, for security of employment, etc.

Despite some limited gains in achieving practical measures of amelioration or material improvement, the working class still lacked an overall political strategy. Too often the working classes were politically exploited or cheated by the middle classes. Werner Sombart described the European revolutions of 1789, 1793, 1830, 1832 and 1848 as fundamentally middle-class movements. He wrote: 'The bourgeoisie used the proletariat as a Jack-in-the-box with which to terrify their opponents—when by its aid they had obtained what they wanted they closed the box and imprisoned Jack once more.'[9] Sombart excepted the Chartists from this charge on the grounds that their demands arose out of the necessities of the proletariat, and one of their foremost aims was to improve the material conditions of the oppressed factory workers,[10] but he charged them with lacking a properly defined socialist programme.

Marx took a somewhat different view of the Chartists' political demands:

> The six points of the Charter which they contend for contain nothing but the demand of universal suffrage, and of conditions without which universal suffrage would be illusory for the working class: such as the ballot, payment of members, annual general elections. But universal suffrage

is the equivalent of political power for the working class of England, where the proletariat forms the large majority of the population, where, in a long, though underground, civil war, it has gained a clear consciousness of its position as a class, and where even the rural districts know no longer any peasants, but only landlords, industrial capitalists (farmers), and hired labourers. The carrying of universal suffrage in England would, therefore, be a far more socialistic measure than anything which has been honoured with that name on the Continent.

Its inevitable result here, is the *political supremacy of the working class.*[11]

Marx, therefore, made more than a grudging admission of the potential efficacy of long-term reformist and parliamentary strategies *in special circumstances.* (He also conceded that important short-term symbolic victories over the bourgeoisie could be won: for example, he regarded the Ten Hour Bill of 1847 as an important working-class victory.[12]) Marx, however, could never bring himself to regard parliamentary reformism as an end in itself, only as an occasionally justified means to revolutionary ends. For Marx, as I have argued in an earlier chapter, became the leading theorist and proponent of revolutionary ideology fashioned deliberately to serve the needs of the proletariat. What Marx evolved was a revolutionary strategy, a programme for the revolutionary working-class movement which was to be the decisive instrument for the fulfilment of Marx's theory of class struggle and proletarian revolution. Only a 'genuinely' revolutionary movement could create the necessary revolutionary consciousness, mobilize the proletariat, wrest political power and control over the means of production from the bourgeoisie, and establish the dictatorship of the proletariat. For Marx, the capitalist system of production, which he anatomized so brilliantly in *Das Kapital,* could not in the long run be 'humanized' and reformed on a piecemeal basis. The naked exploitation of the working class, their reduction to mere dispensable productive units, which Marx saw as the tragic consequence of capitalist market forces, could, he argued passionately, be ended by the ultimate destruction of the bourgeois economic and political system *in toto,* and its replacement by a Communist society.

If the reformist parliamentary strategy of working-class political action ultimately led to working-class promotion of, and participation in, mass parties, the logical alternative revolutionary strategy, as Lenin saw with vivid clarity, is the exclusivist, professionalized revolutionary movement. There are, of course, other major alternatives such as those offered by the anarchist and the syndicalist traditions and ideologies of social movement. Outside late nineteenth-century Russia and Spain, however, anarchist strategies have never gained more than tiny minorities of support among the working classes. On the other hand, syndicalist working-class movements did enjoy considerable mass support in all Western European countries up to the end of the First World War. They are a political movement applying political strategies, for their long-term aim is the abolition of the centralized state and of capitalist and state control in industry. Their industrial action methods have therefore been directed at 'revolutionizing from below' the whole politico-economic framework by establishing a loose federation of worker-controlled industries, services and undertakings. Syndicalism was influential in shaping the policies and strategies of the Social Democratic Federation and the Labour party in Britain, and had important influences on the French and Italian socialist parties. Between the wars some of the most militant syndicalist workers became Communists[13] and the movement survived only as a left-wing sect (though many syndicalist ideas on worker control have been later 'rediscovered' and taken over by anti-Stalinist Marxist groups).

It is possible to distinguish some of the main problems that have confronted each of these three working-class political strategies—the reformist mass party, the revolutionary movement, and worker control—in the context of their attempted implementation in British politics. The enduring major political problems of these strategies and their comparative effect upon each type of strategy and organization certainly reflect many difficulties which are inherent in the articulation of working-class political action in all the heavily industrialized and urbanized Western democracies.

1 *Mass parties.* Professor Duverger employs the concept of 'mass party' to distinguish modern parties with mass memberships from traditionalist 'cadre parties' which are formed on the basis of the politicians' caucus purely for the purpose of filling elective offices.[14] As a typical example of mass party, Duverger cites the French Socialist party:

> In its eyes the recruiting of members is a fundamental

> activity, both from the political and the financial standpoints. In the first place, the party aims at the political education of the working class, at picking out from it an élite capable of taking over the government and the administration of the country: the members are therefore the very substance of the party, the stuff of its activity. Without members, the party would be like a teacher without pupils. Secondly, from the financial point of view, the party is essentially based upon the subscriptions paid by its members . . . This last point is fundamental: every electoral campaign represents considerable expense. The mass-party technique in effect replaces the capitalist financing of electioneering by democratic financing.[15]

Duverger's typologizing is most valuable. Historically, the pioneering working-class socialist parties of the early twentieth century, with their mass memberships, mass participation, democratically determined programmes and subscribing mass memberships, did represent a new organizational form of party, a movement party in the real sense. Clearly, as Duverger suggests, for the traditional cadre parties prior to the granting of universal franchise, 'there could be no question of enrolling the masses at a time when they had no political influence'.[16] Only after the granting of the popular franchise did the cadre parties begin to introduce elements of mass-party organization, such as the National Union in the British Conservative party, and the Birmingham Liberal Caucus in the 1870s or the institution of US party primaries in the early twentieth century.

Here, however, we encounter some of the difficulties involved in Duverger's rather rigid and narrow definition of the cadre and mass parties. Clearly by the mid-twentieth century the British Conservative and Liberal parties had in almost every particular acquired similar 'mass party' features to the British Labour party. But also, in the meantime the latter had acquired at least some of the features of the cadre party. Large trade unions and other socialist organizations continue to make large capital grants to party funds so that the party (to its huge relief one can be sure!) does not have to rely entirely on subscriptions of paid-up members. The party has acquired 'notables' of its own, a durable party élite of senior office holders and elder statesmen enjoying their own not inconsiderable powers of patronage. The Labour party, in common with the trade unions, has not proved immune from the tendencies towards Michels' 'iron law of oligarchy'. Few observers would claim that the mass of card-carrying members expressing themselves either through the agency of National Conference, or through the use of their votes, have succeeded in radically altering or determining the policies of the party leadership.

Clearly, there has been a tendency throughout industrialized competitive party systems towards the displacement of the traditionalist cadre party by the mass party. But, as Jean Blondel argues in a valuable article,[17] the mass party simply cannot be adequately defined in the rigid terms of Duverger, i.e. on the basis that the sole criterion of mass-party membership is paid up and card-carrying subscription.

In the first place, as Blondel points out, there are grave difficulties involved even if we accept this criterion. What percentage of total supporters must be paid-up members for a party to qualify as a mass party? Is one to accept as mass parties all those that throw open card-carrying membership to all citizens? Secondly, there are other possible defining characteristics of the mass party which can provide us with a far more comprehensive and comparatively viable operational definition. As Blondel argues, the mass party is more appropriately defined as a mode of popular 'direct' participation in politics. The people 'link themselves, they associate themselves, to a group known as the political party and owe allegiance to individual leaders because the leaders temporarily represent the political party . . . one should define the mass party as one in which one can find evidence of direct recognition of the abstract notion of party among the followers of the organization.'[18]

Mass parties are therefore based upon popular political movements, that is to say upon normative commitment to, and participation in, political parties. These movements result largely from relatively consistent and durable patterns of popular perception of, and identification with, political parties. Blondel distinguishes six key identifying characteristics of the mass party which are at once both *consequences* of mass party, and the enabling conditions for their survival: 'stability of electoral support'; 'voluntary help in cash or kind'; 'permanent organizations'; 'nationally responsible leadership'; 'access to and utilization of the mass media'; and 'widespread party images'.

In its relationship to these mass parties, the working class is severely handicapped in a number of ways. The first point is that only a minority of the whole working class is politically committed and active. As Richard Hoggart shrewdly points out, many writers on working-class history 'overrate the place of political activity in working-class life' and they 'do not always have an adequate sense of the grass-roots of that life'.[19]

Second, the working class has, as Hoggart puts it, 'had little or no training in the handling of ideas or in analysis'.[20] Certainly, Michael Young's satirical *Meritocracy* is wildly exaggerating when it projects an élite monopoly of intelligence faced by the inept populism of alienated troglodytes. Yet it is true that an increasingly significant tendency of the period since the First World War has been the siphoning off of ever-increasing numbers of talented working-class youth into the meritocratic ladder of higher education and middle-class occupations.

Third, not only is the working class's earnest minority of political activists confronted by a largely apathetic majority among its own people; it is also, as we have seen, ideologically deeply divided. Furthermore, however hard they strive for ideological 'purity', 'solidarity' and organizational 'discipline' among their working-class followers, the leaders of the political working class are constantly faced with the need for compromise and accommodation with the middle-class political minority within the mass-party class coalition. Moreover, these middle-class political activists tend, by the nature of things, to have greater training in intellectual skills, to be more articulate, orally and on paper, and to have the kind of organizational and management skills that enable them to become the dominant element in the mass party leadership. In modern British history this role of the middle classes in building up and largely dominating the mass parties has been a seriously neglected theme, especially in regard to the Labour party.[21]

2 *Proletarian revolution and syndicalism.* It is a pathetic irony that the self-professed movement for the 'true interests' of the working class, the self-proclaimed vanguard of the proletariat, Marxism-Leninism, is not a genuinely working-class movement at all. The very term 'proletariat' is an entirely intellectual invention in no sense derived from working-class life and discourse. All the Marxist-Leninist doctrinal paraphernalia of dialectic, capitalist contradictions and revolutionary consciousness are so many received notions, at best a foreign-sounding glossary of long words which may hoodwink the gullible few but which make the majority of working-class citizens baffled or suspicious. Not only is all the

theory and ideology of Marxist-Leninist Communism invented, articulated and retailed by middle-class intellectuals, but also the middle-class minority of ideological experts forms the leaderships of these movements, all of which are run, with minor variations, basically on the model of the Stalinist party dictatorship, with its 'transmission belt' of commands flowing from a self-perpetuating, bureaucratically entrenched dictatorship at the centre. There are, of course, many working-class members in such movements: indeed they form the majority of the rank and file in the Communist parties of all industrialized nations. Most of these parties, as a matter of course, operate large Communist unions as sub-apparatuses of the party which provide valuable agencies for recruitment and industrial action. But the working-class rank and file are compelled to accept the leadership of the party ideologists and the top party officials.

Because of their character as dictatorial organizations, there is something startlingly irrelevant about some of the recent studies of the working-class grass-roots membership of Communist parties.[22] Of course it is possible to show that many of these members do not appear fully to understand, let alone fully support, party ideology. Naturally, many appear to hold views and prejudices in common with other sectarian socialisms, and with the left wings of the parliamentary socialist parties. Of course, in the face of successive electoral failures and failures to participate in national government, they have found it necessary to show more 'accommodative' tactics and to appear to conform wholeheartedly to methods of parliamentary legality as an expedient tactic. This does not give any grounds for assuming that they have really changed their ideological spots, or that they have abandoned the intention, should they achieve power, of liquidating parliamentary democracy. Lenin revealed the cynical opportunism of the tactic of infiltrating and undermining parliamentary socialist parties with brutal candour when he enjoined British Communists in the 1920s:

> At present the British Communists very often find it hard to approach the masses and even to get a hearing from them. If I come out as a Communist and call upon the workers to vote for Henderson against Lloyd George, they will certainly give me a hearing. And I will be able to explain in a popular manner not only why Soviets are better than parliament and why dictatorship of the proletariat is better than

> the dictatorship of Churchill (disguised by the signboard of bourgeois 'democracy'), but also I want with my vote to support Henderson in the same way as the rope supports a hanged man—that the impending establishment of a government of Hendersons will prove that I am right, will bring over the masses over to my side and will hasten the political death of the Hendersons and the Snowdens just as was the case with their kindred spirits in Russia and Germany.[23]

The tactics of pretending to play the parliamentary game were seen as part of the long-term revolutionary strategy; they were adopted with the specific aim of undermining and destroying the bourgeois democratic 'swindle' which Lenin viewed with such scathing contempt. On all the historical evidence, Marxist-Leninist Communist parties, given the opportunity of power, have never veered from this fundamental opposition to parliamentary democracy.

One of the more fashionable recent explanations for the failure of revolutionary working-class movements to gain strength and political power is the so-called 'embourgeoisement' hypothesis. This is, in a sense, a modern refinement of a powerful traditional line of attack challenging Marx's predictions that the proletariat and the bourgeoisie would become increasingly polarized economically and politically, and that the 'intermediate strata' of lower-middle classes would ultimately be assimilated into the increasingly exploited proletariat. Modern sociological evidence has been marshalled to show that there has been a gradual relative improvement in the living standards and the total income of the working class. It is argued that the working class has become increasingly heterogeneous in levels of skill, types of specialization, and gradations of income and status, and that the better-off members of the working class are therefore becoming merged into the middle class. Some writers also suggest that the increased quality and quantity of social service and social security provision since 1945 has helped the working class compensate for the advantages of job security and fringe benefits traditionally enjoyed by the privileged middle class.

This is not the place to enter the sociological debate as to the soundness or otherwise of this hypothesis. Suffice it to say, however, that if it were shown to be true it would surely follow that there would have been a concomitant decline in the frequency and intensity of working-class industrial militancy, solidarity and action. Yet the very opposite is the case.

Without exception every advanced Western industrial society experienced throughout the late 1960s a resurgence of trade union strikes, unofficial strikes and other forms of workers' industrial action. There has also been a marked resurgence of Trotskyist- and syndicalist-inspired direct action and campaigns for worker control in many industrial countries. In Britain, for example, the Socialist Labour League, a Trotskyist movement which got under way in 1957–58, was considerably strengthened by the adhesion of many British Communist party defectors such as Peter Fryer and Brian Behan who were disillusioned by the Hungarian repression of 1956. Its youth section, the Young Socialists, claimed a membership of approximately 20,000 by late 1969. Its industrial arm, the *All Trades Union Alliance*, has been involved in instigating and encouraging a very large number of strikes, especially in the automobile, dock and engineering industries. Nor do the revolutionary Marxist groups show any propensity for reconciling themselves to modern-style productivity agreements. Tony Cliff, theorist of the Marxist International Socialists, has written a guide aimed at undermining such 'bourgeois swindles' which he clearly angles to a shop-steward readership. He bluntly advocates four alternative strategies to defeat the employers' offensive: outright refusal to accept parts of a signed deal; repudiation of a deal; pressure to renegotiate sections of a deal 'under the threat of industrial action'; and deliberate misinterpretation of parts of the agreement.[24]

The persistence and militancy of movements of working-class action would seem, clearly, to contradict the embourgeoisement hypothesis. Serge Mallet's sociological study, *La nouvelle classe ouvrière* (1963), provides a valuable approach to this problem. He shows that, although the worker as consumer has begun to acquire a certain affluence and has become in some ways indistinguishable from the consumers of the middle class, the distinctiveness of his relationships at work, the tensions and discomforts of his productive situation, remain a constant source of friction with the employers. In the factory, the worker still feels compelled to engage in traditional trade union and workers' action in order to defend his 'class interest' as a worker. This readiness to resort to collective industrial action, however, should not be confused with the conception of a generally shared and agreed working-class political ideology or even agreed collective economic aims. *Ad hoc* industrial action is more accurately understood as a kind of pragmatic 'instrumental collectivism' (to borrow a term from Goldthorpe and Lockwood[25]) rather than as the unfolding of a planned revolutionary strategy.

However much revolutionaries attempt to exploit it, working-class action seems likely to remain stubbornly spontaneous, spasmodic and politically uncoordinated and inconsistent, essentially unresponsive to the demands of grandiose revolutionary strategy.

Revolutionary and totalitarian movements

My concern here is with the political strategies and organizational forms of revolutionary movements, and not with the voluminous literature on revolutionary ideologies and history or with general theories of revolution.

Revolutionary movements are aimed at sweeping away existing political, economic or social structures. Some are concerned with the promotion of new structures and relationships to be established in place of the old; others have no such ideological commitment or pretensions and take the form of a purely destructive *antipolitik*, directed at bringing the pillars of social order crashing down.

Clearly, as we have observed earlier in our review of types of movement, many 'reformist', populist and millenarist movements adopt the language and doctrine of revolution, though they may often quail at the prospect of implementing revolution, and many pathetically fail to acquire the necessary organization, manpower, or *matériel* to implement a revolutionary strategy. The distinction between reformist and revolutionary movements is blurred still further in the fact that many initially reformist or protest movements can move across into the revolutionary camp. For example, movements of populist discontent, working-class action, and campaigns for racial and ethnic rights, can be very dramatically 'radicalized' either as the result of further repression or exploitation by the authorities, or because a moderate leadership is displaced by revolutionaries.

1 *Guerrilla-based revolution.* One of the great, possibly decisive, strengths of modern revolutionary movements in Third World countries has been their ability (as, for example, in China, Algeria and Cuba) to establish a firm foundation of popular support among the rural poor. This base is vital to the successful operation of a guerrilla revolution: it ensures, because of its

entirely autochthonous character, the vital supply of manpower, aid and succour, and invaluable secure retreats and weapons' dumps. Such guerrilla-mounted operations can take place in perfect camouflage with the tacit or active collaboration of the bulk of the population, right under the noses of the guerrillas' enemies.

The guerrilla strategy, however, is not limited in applicability to economically underdeveloped Third World situations. The experiences of the French *Maquis* and Jugoslav partisans, for example, are a useful reminder of the value of the strategy in the conduct of a liberation struggle against a heavily-armed occupying army. There have been many attempts to apply guerrilla strategy and tactics in an urban setting. Urban guerrillas, however, lack the vital security of isolated rural retreats and fastnesses: they have nowhere safe to lick their wounds, to train new recruits or to make contact with external allies. They can, of course, achieve considerable long-term harassment of security forces by terrorization, armed attacks, sabotage and by tricking and evading the police and the military deployed by the regime. These tactics may, as the 1969–70 riots in Belfast and Derry showed, result in a virtual state of military occupation and partial, recurrent seige, especially where the security forces and the government are inhibited in their response capacity by constitutional, judicial and humanitarian constraints. This gives considerable scope, as Black Power rioters in US cities have discovered, for hit-and-run actions against the authorities. But this does not mean that urban guerrilla activity is an adequate strategy for making a political revolution.

The sacrifice and heroic courage of those who rose in the Warsaw Ghetto against the Nazis was tragic proof that even the most determined and desperate attempt by an urban-based liberation movement could not hold out against the superior technology and firing power of a ruthless occupying force which was prepared to liquidate all who stood in its way.

On the other hand, despite the increased technical resources of security forces and military units set against them, rural-based guerrilla revolutionary movements continue, as in Vietnam, to be remarkably resilient, indeed almost indestructible, against the most powerful modern armies. The proviso should be added, however (again, as illustrated in Vietnam) that some form of external aid, weapons, personnel and food supplies, and a degree of external ideological and military support are necessary for the continuance of full-scale, guerrilla-based revolutionary war.

One important point to note is that a clear-cut ideology or an elaborate set of revolutionary principles or doctrines is not a prerequisite for effective guerrilla-based revolution. It is true that the Chinese Communist Party adopted such doctrines (though they were largely derivative from Marxist-Leninist and Stalinist tutelage), but it could hardly be claimed that the Algerian guerrilla fighters had any such shared doctrines in common. And in the case of Cuba, we have sound evidence that Castro and his handful of guerrilla fighters in the Sierra Maestra in 1957 had no revolutionary ideology to speak of at all: they were certainly not Marxists, and Castro and his followers only began to profess a rather selective adherence to Marxism-Leninism in order to gain vital Soviet bloc aid in the face of America's economic blockade of Cuba.[26]

Indeed guerrilla revolutionary movements' doctrines and policies, both before and after the seizure of power, are more generally moulded by the whims and declarations of their charismatic leaders. If there are any common principles shared by successful guerrilla movements in general, they boil down to a vague anti-colonialist policy and adherence to the basic strategic principles of successful guerrilla combat which Ché Guevara defines as constant mobility, constant distrust and constant vigilance. The fact that these principles have also informed the policies of guerrilla revolutionary movements in power helps to explain their extraordinary adaptive pragmatism and their lack of ideological consistency.

2 *Revolutionary conspiracies of secret societies*. The style of revolution almost the polar opposite to the mass uprising of the ill-armed poor is the palace *putsch*, or cabinet coup of a handful of notables, powerful military officers or ministers, a seizure of control over the organs of government at the top. Such revolutionary strategies may still be very effective in, for example, relatively unstable regimes in South America, Central Africa and the Middle East, and they frequently have revolutionary consequences. But they are not normally, or necessarily, the work of revolutionary movements. Popular participation and support is not always welcome when all that is sought is a change in top personnel or policy, combined with the retention of dictatorship.

The secret conspiratorial societies which were such a notable feature of European politics between 1789 and 1848 were, as Hobsbawm has pointed out,[27] a very important embryonic form of revolutionary social movement. These societies developed the most elaborate formalities of initiation, ceremonial, oath-taking and symbolism, so that they became 'often ritualized to the point of resembling an Italian opera'.[28]

Closely linked with Masonic groups, these societies were generally run by *émigrés* based in such cities as Geneva, Brussels and London, and often engaged in international and supra-national conspiracy. Classic examples are: the Jacobin societies; the Irish Fenian Brotherhood, active from the 1820s onwards; the League of Outlaws (1834), an organization of German *émigrés*; the Jacobin and Blanquist revolutionary brotherhoods.

What were the key features of these conspiratorial societies? First, their stress on the exclusiveness of their societies, and their duty of absolute secrecy and loyalty. Second, all members had a duty to infiltrate and influence other organizations, acting as agents of their own brotherhoods. Third, it was the aim of these movements to establish small dedicated cadres which would be in a position to take advantage of revolutionary turbulence by stimulating armed risings, and, possibly, by seizing political control for the brotherhood.

These societies have tended to imitate each other's methods. The traditions and methods of the conspiratorial society can be traced through the Conspiracy of Equals, the Jacobins and the Blanquist groups in France, down to the Russian populists, Lenin's revolutionary party, and such contemporary movements as the Ku Klux Klan, the I.R.A. and the Black Panthers. This does not mean that the features of very small membership, Ruritanian rituals and somewhat amateurish organization have always been retained. These movements often underwent considerable rationalization and modernization before developing into mass revolutionary parties or movements. Hobsbawm, for example, cites the excellent example of the League of Communists, which developed, largely through Marx's influence, into a centralized democratic organization, having originated as a conspiratorial society of German *émigrés*.

3 *The Leninist strategy*. Lenin's theory and practice of revolution was based on three major elements. First was his implacable hostility towards the whole politico-economic structure of the autocratic government of Russia, and towards the global capitalist system. (This hostility was both augmented and intensified as a result of Lenin's adherence to Marxist doctrines and theories of class struggle and revolution.) Second, Lenin was acutely aware of

the popular grievances of the masses of peasants, demoralized conscripts and industrial workers in pre-revolutionary Russia. What is more, he realized that any revolutionary movement would have to appeal to the needs and desires of the masses if it was to acquire the necessary base of popular support to seize control of the state. Third, and equally vital to his success, Lenin realized that the democratic mass parties and trade unions of the Social Democratic model were too unwieldy and ideologically and organizationally amorphous to provide a determined, ruthless revolutionary instrument for seizing political power.

Lenin saw that he must have a party in which there was near-perfect discipline, absolute loyalty and absolute obedience to the orders of the party leadership, and unveering dedication to the aim of capturing power. That is why he held out against Martov and the Mensheviks at the second Congress of the Russian Social Democrats (1903). Martov wanted to open the doors of Social Democratic party membership to all sympathizers. Lenin would have none of this: he wanted an 'exclusivist' party of hand-picked, carefully trained, totally disciplined and dedicated revolutionaries. His image of the ideal party member vividly recalls Bakunin and Nechaev's *The Catechism of a Revolutionist*:

> He has only one idea: the revolution; and he has broken with all the laws and codes of morals of the educated world. He lives in it only to destroy it the more surely; everything in it must be equally hateful to him. He must be cold: he must be ready to die, he must train himself to bear torture, and he must be ready to kill in himself any sentiment, including that of honour, the moment it interferes with his purpose.[29]

Lenin spelt out his uncompromising model of the revolutionary movement in the pamphlet, *What Is To Be Done?* (1902). The framework he laid down inevitably became the design for the Bolshevik party in Russia. Lenin summarized his main organizational principles very neatly:

> I assert: 1) that no revolutionary movement can endure without a stable organization of leaders that maintains continuity: 2) that the wider the masses spontaneously drawn into the struggle, forming the basis of the movement and participating in it, the more urgent the need of such an organization, and the more solid this organization must be

> (for it is much easier for demagogues to sidetrack the more backward sections of the masses); 3) that such an organization must consist chiefly of people professionally engaged in revolutionary activity; 4) that in an autocratic state, the more we *confine* the membership of such an organization to people who are professionally engaged in revolutionary activity and who have been professionally trained in the art of combating the political police, the more difficult will it be to wipe out such an organization, and, 5) the *greater* will be the number of people of the working class and of the other classes of society who will be able to join the movement and perform active work in it.[30]

Lenin's conception of the exclusive, disciplined, professional, revolutionary organization under strict centralized control stems directly, therefore, from the tradition of the conspiratorial secret society. He saw such an *organization* as something essentially distinct from, and superior to, the mass revolutionary *movement*. The party organization was to be the carefully tuned machine that would be the vital activator, co-ordinator and manipulator of the anti-political grievances, resentments and alienations which are the elements of potential mass revolutionism. Both organization and movement were vital to the success of Lenin's strategy, but he was confident that the party, with its self-professed monopoly of truth about the past, present and future of the revolution, would be able to *induce* from above the prerequisite mass revolutionary consciousness. One of Lenin's most original contributions as a strategist and practitioner of a revolutionary movement was his refinement of the techniques of mass manipulation. The general outline of his ideas in *What Is To Be Done?* prefigures much of the theoretical and practical work of the Soviet Communist Party which was developed by Lenin and was later refined by Stalin into an instrument of totalitarian control:

> The active and widespread participation of the masses will not suffer; on the contrary, it will benefit by the fact that a 'dozen' experienced revolutionaries, trained professionally no less than the police, will centralize all the secret aspects of the work—drawing up leaflets, working out approximate plans and appointing bodies of leaders for each urban district, for each factory district and for each educational institution, etc. . . . The centralization of the most secret

> functions in an organization of revolutionaries will not diminish, but rather increase the extent and quality of the activity of a large number of other organizations which are intended for a broad public and are therefore as loose and non-secret as possible, such as workers' trade unions, workers' self-education circles and circles for reading illegal literature, socialist and also democratic circles among other sections of the population; etc.[31]

The totalitarian character of the Leninist, and later the Stalinist, model Communist party organization was inevitably exported to all countries where Soviet Marxism-Leninism sought either to establish new revolutionary parties or to take over existing ones. The model was imposed at bayonet-point on Eastern European countries signed away to Stalin's 'sphere of influence' after 1945.

In the context of the Leninist theory of revolutionary movement, an authoritative and comprehensive party ideology becomes a clear organizational necessity. It is the means by which the centralized party organization derives its goals, its guidelines to conduct, and an orientation to the world of conflicting and ambiguous movements and ideas which the party is constantly seeking to subdue and control. But the party ideology is far more than this: it is the dogmatically imposed 'faith and fount' of the ideal party member's total commitment to the cause of the revolution.

The party's ruthless organizational expediencies have been most effectively demonstrated and analysed by studies such as that of Philip Selznick and many others.[32] Yet it would be quite wrong to assume, on the basis of all the evidence about what Selznick calls 'the organizational weapon' of Bolshevism, that therefore the long-term revolutionary ideological goals are simply so much irrelevant window-dressing for all party members. Hannah Arendt has written in the same breath of Hitler's entourage and the Bolshevik Politburo: 'To them ideological clichés are mere devices to organize the masses, and they feel no compunction about changing them according to the needs of circumstances if only the organizational principle is kept intact.'[33] But the tragic paradox of revolutionary movement is surely that it commits some of its most inhuman crimes in the fanatical belief that the movement's visions of 'perfect society', however warped they may appear to outside observers, can be *physically* realized. Thus, it was possible for a fanatical Nazi to believe he was serving the highest purposes of humanity through the creation of a Thousand Year Reich of 'the super-race' and the degradation of 'inferior races'; and individual Soviet Communists could, and still do, believe that they are working for a great classless society and the final emancipation of the world proletariat.

It is interesting to note the similarities in the *means* of mass revolutionism adopted by Stalinist Communism and Nazism although they were not, as has so often been implied,[34] identical phenomena. Both movements were prepared to use legal electoral contests as an opportunist strategy while secretly conspiring to use illegality and force to bludgeon their way into power. Both movements developed the full panoply of a secret police terror apparatus. All the instruments of indoctrination, blackmail, forced 'confessions', show trials, labour camps and genocide, which Stalin deployed, were also used by Hitler with even deadlier ferocity and sadism. But in the case of Nazism *all* the supporters of Nazism, *all* participants in the mass revolutionism of the movement were constantly being stimulated and exhorted to exalt the use of terror, persecution and unspeakable degradation against the Jews and other 'non-Aryan' people: all Nazis became involved in living and promoting the monstrous myth of the 'master race' and the service of the Führer. For this reason the committal of Nazi crimes against humanity was not confined, as in the case of Stalin's regime, to decision-making party chiefs, secret police members, labour camp gaolers and the rest of the parasitic gangsterism of totalitarian dictatorship. Under Hitler, Nazi crime corrupted a large part of the whole German nation who actively abetted its perpetration. Nazism, unlike Bolshevism, contrived to possess a whole people by its evil.

4 *Mass revolutionism.* Features of the strategy of mass revolutionism have been keenly emulated among a wide range of racial, student and neo-Marxist movements. Stokely Carmichael and Charles Hamilton, for example, in their attempt to formulate an ideology of 'liberation' for the Black Power movement[35] in the United States, follow this strategy in many significant respects. There is, of course, the implacable hatred of the 'system' (which they designate a racist, white society), and the call to destroy the 'system'. As means to that end they wish to create a 'new consciousness' among Negroes nourished on the language of 'struggle' and images of 'liberation'. They wish to inculcate an atmosphere of desperate crisis, to persuade their fellow Negroes that the

revolutionary moment has come and they had better wake up to it. Because the situation is, in their view, desperate for Negroes in America, they are prepared to risk violence and to make thinly-veiled threats of violence and revenge: 'In the end, we cannot and shall not offer any guarantees that Black Power, if achieved, would be non-racist . . . The final truth is that the white society is not entitled to reassurances even if it were possible to offer them.'[36] 'They [a rapidly growing body of black people] will not be stopped in their drive to achieve dignity, to achieve their share of power, indeed to become their own men and women—in this time and in this land—*by whatever means necessary*.'[37]

If one substitutes in each case 'capitalist', 'imperialism' and 'US militarism' in place of 'white society' as targets for destruction one recognizes the universal slogans of contemporary student and neo-Marxist revolutionisms of the late 1960s.

Mass revolutionisms that fail to develop any counterbalancing stable leadership or organizational centre frequently run out of control. They may lapse into myriad sectarian conflicts and rivalries. Alternatively, unless suppressed, they can develop a momentum of purge, counter-purge and general turbulence and dislocation sufficient totally to disrupt normal conditions of life, production and administration. It was, for example, as a consequence of the excesses of the Red Guards, whom Mao himself had stimulated into action in the Chinese Great Proletarian Cultural Revolution, 1965–69, that the People's Liberation Army had to be called in to provide some guarantee of protection of the dislocated party bureaucracy and to facilitate a return to minimal economic and political stability. Overstimulated, mass revolutionism can reach the level of a collective psychic disorder with extremely damaging social consequences.

The anarchist movements,[38] which were an important minority within the revolutionary tradition from the early nineteenth century right down to the 1920s, constitute an extreme anti-political, putative mass revolutionism. Anarchism remained a quasi-mass movement, to the intense disappointment of leading anarchists, despite the enormous intellectual influence of anarchist writers and artists, and in spite of the determined efforts of anarchist strongholds in, for example, late nineteenth-century Russia and Spain from the early 1900s to the Civil War.[39] As a popular movement, anarchism failed to develop a mass base of support in any of the advanced industrial countries. It was at once too romantic and impractical in its doctrines and tactics to begin to compete with the more elaborate socialist and Fascist movements, which at least purported to offer positive political solutions to meet the demands of the urban masses. Anarchism remained, therefore, in part a minority intellectual sect, and in part a style of rural populist protest increasingly beleaguered, and ultimately overwhelmed, by the twentieth-century social changes.

5 *Fascist movements.* Even if he were to consult the vast output of books and articles that have attempted to interpret, explain and anatomize Fascism,[40] the student could be forgiven if he were to finish up more baffled and confused than ever about what Fascism really is, and what it really means to label with this term a wide variety of movements that arose to the peak of their strength between 1930 and 1945.

The original Fascist movement was that of Mussolini in Italy. It was started during the First World War and acquired a hotchpotch of ideas and slogans which were to have a popular appeal among people hit by post-war disillusion and the poverty of the depression, and somewhat resentful of Italy's second-class status as a European power. It was ultra-patriotic, ultra-nationalist and pro-militarist in policy and style. Italian Fascism was to some extent revolutionary: in its desire to shake off the constraints of bourgeois liberal democratic values and practices; in its dedication to modernization and industrial growth; and in its exaltation of the role of youth. In other respects it was counter-revolutionary and reactionary: Mussolini offered the capitalists and the Church a bulwark against Bolshevism; the whole style and practice of Fascism favoured the continuance of the privileges and statuses of the Italian monarchy and aristocracy, and the whole structure of Fascist rule was rigidly élitist; and there was the flagrant latter-day colonialism of Mussolini, which was directly counter-revolutionary in the context of the mounting global colonial emancipationist movement of the period.

Mussolini's Black Shirts had many imitators throughout Europe and Latin America,[41] though there were enormous variations in ideology and programme. It was not, however, the rather threadbare ideas of Italian Fascism that proved so appealing (though certainly ultra-nationalism and anti-Bolshevism became identifying characteristics of all Fascisms), but rather its mass revolutionist techniques. Mussolini, drawing freely on his experience as a socialist party organizer and propagandist, proved able to use the techniques of the mass movement with enormous *élan* and propaganda success. He learned how to use the symbolism and ritual of para-military organizations, uniforms, mass parades, demonstration and the whole paraphernalia of youth movement and media manipulation, to consolidate his personal charisma and political power as dictator. In the long process of this consolidation, between 1921 and 1928, the inherent ambiguities and internal contradictions of Fascism became apparent.

There was a running conflict over political aims and methods between the Fascist movement's grass-roots militants and members of Mussolini's para-military *Militia*, and the more conservative traditionalist forces in Italy which Mussolini was not powerful enough to destroy or control and upon whose tacit support the Mussolini regime depended for its survival. These were the army, the Church, the monarchy, large landowners and the major capitalist interests. There was, furthermore, an internal conflict within the Fascist movement between the impetuous revolutionary zeal of the mass movement and the needs of the movement-regime to establish a stable, disciplined and centrally controlled party bureaucracy. There is evidence that not only the Fascist movement organizers, but also Mussolini himself, became confused, baffled and vacillating, in the search for a Fascist political strategy in the mid 1920s, on the eve of the 'second wave' of Fascist illegality and intimidation.[42]

The other European Fascisms by no means followed the Italian historical pattern, in many respects. This, however, does not mean that we should abandon the term Fascism. All these movements combined, to some degree, mass revolutionist strategies with reactionary ideologies compounded of virulent ultra-nationalism, exaltation of irrationality, illegality, violence and fanatical anti-Communism. In Spain, the Falange only became temporarily dominant in the right-wing coalition of the 'national movement' between 1936 and 1941–42. During this period, its ideological militancy and its sympathy with its brother movements, Nazism and Italian Fascism, was of indispensable value in acquiring the resources for Franco's Civil War victory. By the 1950s the old ideological fanaticism of the Falange was an embarrassment to the Spanish regime and the Falange is now almost totally excluded from influence over the regime's policy.

Spanish and Italian Fascisms also lacked the *volkisch* racialist and anti-Semitic ideology of Hitler's Nazism. (Italian Fascism managed to avoid anti-Semitic persecution on a major scale until the SS itself directly intervened under the German occupation.[43]) Furthermore, Hitler was vastly more successful both in his use of mass revolutionist strategies, mass propaganda and party organization and in his control of mass communications media, nationalist symbolism and slogans. He appealed to German youth and to the German propensities for authoritative dictatorial government and military glory, and to the German desire for revenge against the humiliations imposed by the Versailles powers. Hitler used the full repertoire of mass revolutionism both to further his racialist aims of pathological anti-Semitism and to bolster his own charisma and power as leader of the new 'revolution'. Through the agency of the Nazi para-military terror organizations, both the SA and the SS and later the Gestapo, the Hitler regime was able to indulge in violent and sadistic mass terrorism, mass liquidation, racial persecution and racial extermination, secure in the knowledge that all popular bases of organized mass political opposition had been eliminated within the first twelve months of the Nazi revolution in 1933. Despite the considerable evidence, authoritatively marshalled by Professor Bracher,[44] that Hitler continued to meet stiff resistance to his will among individual members of the top military and state bureaucracy, the overwhelming actual and potential power over German society which fell to the Nazi party, passed the threshold of totalitarianism appallingly rapidly after 1933. In Spain, Italy, Rumania and Hungary, Fascist movements, despite their considerable influence as mass movements, never achieved the scale of the Nazi hegemony.

6 *Totalitarian movement*. However totalitarian their ambitions and style of organization, movements can, of course, only implement totalitarianism, that is to say the calculated destruction of all rival parties, loyalties and potential bases of opposition, when they have accomplished revolutionary seizure of power.

However, while totalitarian policies can attempt the prevention of any new and potentially dangerous spontaneous movement within their frontiers (with the technological and police resources of modern totalitarianisms this repression can be comprehensive and effective), this does not mean that the totalitarian leadership can dispense with its own movement. On the contrary, it becomes increasingly valuable to leaders. Even a totalitarian regime cannot dispense with the need for widespread and willing participation at all levels of the civil and military administration, in industry, among the intellectuals and scientific experts, etc. It is necessary that the motivation of all these personnel be kept at a high level, in order that their allegiance and commitment to the regime and their general morale should be sustained. The movement is the most effective and, indeed, the sole remaining, organ which the leadership has available for the purposes of acquiring popular legitimation and support.

Totalitarian regimes, therefore, devour all but their own movements: these they cannot afford to kill. They may purge them of whole generations of leaders, they may reverse or severely alter their policies, allegiances and external political alignments, but their party organizations must continue to wage a constant struggle to maintain movement bases of popular support, and having sustained them, to keep tight party control over them. The costs to the regime of maintaining strict control and surveillance over their movements and their youth, cultural, workers' and peasants' auxiliaries, must be added to the enormous costs of propaganda dissemination and the heavy investment in mass indoctrination, especially of youth, which is characteristic of all totalitarian states. These costs are met because the totalitarian regime knows that the best form of psychological and ideological defence against all external and anti-totalitarian influences is attack, and because it is vital to prepare successive generations for the possibility of military service for the regime. Thus, North Korean Communist party workers proudly show foreign visitors lines of four- to six-year-old children waiting their turn at kindergarten 'to go and stab a cardboard image of an American soldier with toy guns'.[45]

The mass movement basis of totalitarianism is, therefore, the essential means by which the totalitarian *nation* is welded together, and to the regime: it is the creator of the will which enables the regime to survive. And just because the movement is constantly engaged in sustaining ideological commitment, in communicating the charisma and charismatic symbols of the revolution, and in maintaining participation in the party and its satellite organizations, especially among the young, it is the least predictable and least understood element in totalitarianism so far as outside observers are concerned. Even the leaders of the regime cannot really accurately gauge the effect and strength of movement commitment and participation among the people. There is an internal dialectic between the movement created by charisma and indoctrination, and the institutionalized party bureaucracy which strives to manipulate the masses. It is thus very misleading and inaccurate to assume, because of the pragmatic and accommodative capacity often demonstrated by the leaders and hierarchies of the party bureaucracies in their dealings with the outside world, that therefore the movement is dying or becoming 'deradicalized'.[46] This is to confuse the party's organizational bureaucracy with the movement. The powers of the totalitarian movement to influence, to believe in, and to serve its leaders over considerable periods have been proven historically. Like secular religions, their ideologies and principles have a frequently underrated power to remould human consciousness, to recharge constantly the revolutionary spirit of the masses, and to provide the movement with a momentum of its own which may only be halted by a more appealing counter-movement or by total defeat in war.

Conclusion: Moral Dilemmas of Social Movement

The most important problems human beings confront when faced with the collective actions of others, or with the desire to initiate collective actions, are essentially moral. It is not possible for us to choose the perfect form of collective action designed to our individual specification. All varieties of social movement constitute alternative strategies of collective action aimed at achieving various alternative goals, and they employ different methods and interventions in social life in support of these goals.

If we are to combine successfully to achieve any social objective, whether this be orderly government, an improvement in the condition of the world's poor, the ending of nuclear weapon testing, or the preservation of ancient monuments, one thing is certain: we must adopt some form of collective action. Social objectives cannot be agreed or implemented without social movement. Faced with the alternatives of social inaction or the absence of collaborative action, and some form of social movement, the latter is for most human beings the lesser of two evils.

But what kind of social movement should be adopted? Many have the impression that movements are inevitably violent and destructive in their effects. They are obsessed with the images of revolutionary street fighting, tear-gas and civil strife, and with what Christopher Booker has called the *Neophiliacs*, movements of minorities who become victims of collective fantasies, the excesses of drug-orgies and cults, and the lunatic fringes of sexual liberation movements. This is a totally unbalanced image of social movement, a concentration on the frothy trivia of newsworthy crankiness and sensationalism.

Social movement, used as a working concept in the sense defined in this discussion, embraces a vast number of collective endeavours which have been serious, creative, and responsible in the fullest sense. Heberle has written forcefully of the creative role of movements: 'If the dominant minority in a society is unwilling to make the necessary adjustments [for society to survive], these will have to be achieved . . . by a social movement. In this kind of situation a social movement is the force which saves the society from destruction, although the dominant minority may not realize it at the time.'[1]

Faced with the paradox that humanity, which has combined to achieve greater unity, greater understanding, and a better human community, has also collectively achieved genocide, persecution, and bitter social conflict and suffering, how is one to distinguish the creative and constructive elements of social movement? Unless we play gods ourselves we cannot finally and definitively hand out the prizes at some kind of historical judgement day. All social movement is inevitably imperfect and it is impossible even for the most careful historian or social scientist to apportion blame precisely to those responsible for actions which meet with his disapproval.

The most valuable studies of social movements are judicious and cautious in their treatment of the historical evidence, fully aware of the moral dilemmas involved in all collective actions, and compassionate towards the participants and their problems. They will, against this background of humane understanding, truthfully strive to interpret and *understand* the ideas, policies and actions of the movement concerned.

Implicitly, I hope some of the virtues of the ideal student and researcher of social movement will have emerged from this introductory review. He is meticulous over historical detail and background, modest and tentative in his approach to analysis, and suspicious of strident and dogmatic generalization. Above all, he will have the imaginative insight and humanity to place himself in another's situation: even in the case of a social movement whose aims he finds instinctively unsympathetic he will constantly remind himself, 'There, in different circumstances in a different time and place, but for the Grace of God, go I.'

But if it is good for the historian and sociologist to be reminded that men are often moulded by movements as well as by the pressures and events of their times, it is also salutary for practitioners of social movement to recall that movements are made by men. Within the physical constraints of ignorance, scarcity, natural disaster and foreign conquest, the individual movement leaders and participants are individuals with free will. They are challenged constantly to make moral choices and to take responsibility, within the framework of collective action, for decisions that may affect the lives of dozens, hundreds or even millions of fellow human-beings.

It is, therefore, not only the choices of great leaders which may be decisive, but, just as important, the choices of thousands of the rank-and-file humanity who have the moral responsibility for deciding whether they will join or support a given collective action, how they will select their programmes and leaders, what means they are prepared to employ to realize the movement's aims, and so forth.

There is no doubt that the response to the challenges posed by the moral dilemmas of collective action often calls for enormous moral courage and heroic self-sacrifice. I would wish to be more positive and claim that society has a great need for movement practitioners, leaders and active participants, devoted to the service of great ideals reflecting abiding and fundamental human needs. Such needs include: distributive justice, that is, a radical redistribution of global wealth to the poverty-stricken and underprivileged; racial equality, harmony and dignity; conservation of global natural resources and wild-life against the poisoning and pollution resulting from the application of human science; the establishment of a peaceful international order; and the preservation of individual rights and liberties under the rule of law.

It might reasonably be objected that the realization of any one of these aims would require an intellectual leadership commanding the science and technology of both the USA and the USSR and a political theory of even greater innovative brilliance than that of Classical Greece. Nevertheless, it is to be hoped that the social movements of the future will not be paralysed into inaction by the extent of the political and organizational problems that face them.

As to the methods that might be adopted by future social movements, it is probable that the desperation and nihilistic destructiveness of mass revolutionist movements and revolutionist conflicts will intensify as political and social élites show continuing failure in their attempts to grapple with the social, physical and political problems, such as the population explosion, the continuation of international conflict, and the increase of serious chemical pollution. And this type of protest is likely to become increasingly transnational.

There are, however, classic strategies of social movement other than instant protest demonstration and riot. The great religious, reformist and moral crusade movements of the past managed, as we have seen, to combine desperate moral concern with a non-violent but tremendously creative style of movement built upon rational discussion, rational persuasion, the drafting of practicable and constructive programmes and legislative action. Contemporary portraits and descriptions of participants in early reform campaigns such as the factory reform movement and the anti-slavery society reveal the impressively diligent attention and deep commitment accorded to these causes. The whole spirit of such reformist movements was dedicated and determined; their aims were revolutionary by the standards of the time; their methods were outstandingly realistic, intelligent, practical and effective. Today there is the contemporary example of the movement for European unity, the culmination of which may be the establishment of a United States of Europe. These are the kinds of social movement that can bridge the gaps between élites and non-élites, and such movements, capable of informed, intelligent, concerted action on an international scale, are a desperate need for a world in which failure to resolve dilemmas of social conflict may result in the total destruction of society.

Notes and References

1/ Concepts of Social Movement

1 "One of No Party", *Random Recollections of the House of Commons from the Years 1830– close of 1835*, London 1836, p. 63.
2 William Cobbett, *Political Register*, July 25, 1812.
3 Thomas Carlyle, *Works*, Vol. II, pp. 234–6.
4 Charles Dickens, *Pickwick Papers*, p. 13.
5 Raymond Williams, *Culture and Society, 1750–1950*, Penguin Books, Harmondsworth 1961, pp. 287–8.
6 T. D. Weldon, *The Vocabulary of Politics*, Penguin Books, Harmondsworth 1955.
7 It would be wrong to assume that such 'collective migrations' are entirely a thing of the past. In the winter of 1969–70 it was reported that a large group of French-speaking immigrants to Canada, living in Quebec, planned to migrate *en masse* to S. Alberta. The group called itself L'Association des Immigrants Francophone (AIF), and proposed to form an agricultural co-operative community. Report in *The Times*, London, January 4, 1970. See also scholarly discussion in A. H. Richmond, "The Sociology of Migration", in *Migration*, edited by J. A. Jackson, Cambridge University Press, London 1970.
8 Review of E. J. Hobsbawm and George Rudé's *Captain Swing*, Lawrence and Wishart, London 1969, in *Times Literary Supplement*, September 11, 1969.
9 Bryan Wilson (ed.), *Patterns of Sectarianism: Organization and Ideology in Social and Religious Movements*, Heinemann, London 1967, p. 2.
10 Hannah Arendt, *The Burden of Our Time*, Secker and Warburg, London 1951, pp. 249 and 251.
11 E. H. Carr, *What is History?* Penguin Books, Harmondsworth 1964, p. 50.
12 Lorenz von Stein, *The History of the Social Movement in France, 1789–1850*, edited and translated by Dr K. Mengelberg, Bedminster Press, Totowa, New Jersey 1964; the quotation is from the editor's introduction, p. 6.
13 Ibid., p. 51.
14 Ibid., p. 55.
15 Werner Sombart, *Socialism and the Social Movement*, first English translation, Dent, London 1909, p. 2.
16 Ibid., p. 10.
17 Ferdinand Tönnies, *Community and Association*, Routledge and Kegan Paul, London, pp. 25–6.
18 Ibid., p. 23.
19 Ibid., p. 23.
20 Ibid., p. 23.
21 Rudolf Heberle, *Social Movements: An Introduction to Political Sociology*, Appleton-Century-Crofts Inc., New York 1951, p. 2.

22 Ibid., p. 8.
23 Ibid., p. 14.
24 Ibid., p. 15.
25 Ibid., p. 7.
26 Herbert Blumer, "Collective Behaviour", in *Review of Sociology: Analysis of a Decade*, edited by Gittler, Wiley, New York 1957, p. 145.
27 Neil J. Smelser, *Theory of Collective Behaviour*, Routledge and Kegan Paul, London 1962, p. 14.
28 Ibid., p. 313.
29 For an account of the spontaneous element in Scout movement development see Paul Wilkinson, "English Youth Movements 1908–1930", in *Journal of Contemporary History*, Vol. 4, No. 2, April 1969, pp. 3–23.
30 W. J. M. Mackenzie, *Politics and Social Science*, Penguin Books, Harmondsworth 1967, p. 377.

2/ Rousseau, Marx and Movement

1 See J. C. Rees, "Lenin and Marxism", in *Lenin: the Man, the Theorist, the Leader*, edited by L. Schapiro and P. Reddaway, Pall Mall Press, London 1967, pp. 87–105, which cogently argues that Lenin's Marxist belief was sincerely held and that it was the decisive intellectual influence upon his career and revolutionary leadership.
2 Shlomo Avineri, *The Social and Political Thought of Karl Marx*, Cambridge University Press, London 1968, p. 251.
3 Friedrich Engels' Preface to the 1886 English Edition, *Capital*, Progress Publishers, Moscow 1965, p. 5.
4 Locke, Hume, Rousseau, *Social Contract*, World Classics Edition, Oxford University Press, London 1947, p. 245.
5 Ibid., p. 246.
6 Ibid., p. 255.
7 Ibid., p. 274.
8 Ibid., p. 274.
9 Ibid., p. 289.
10 Ibid., p. 261.
11 Ibid., p. 275.
12 Ibid., p. 283.
13 For example: Isaiah Berlin, *Karl Marx*, Oxford University Press, London 1960; Shlomo Avineri, *The Social and Political Thought of Karl Marx*, Cambridge University Press, London 1968; Sidney Hook, *Marx and the Marxists: The Ambiguous Legacy*, Princeton University Press, Princeton, New Jersey 1955; Bertram D. Wolfe, *Marxism: One Hundred Years in the Life of a Doctrine*, Chapman and Hall, London 1967.
14 Marx to Weydemeyer, March 5, 1852, *Karl Marx and Frederick Engels Selected Correspondence*, Foreign Languages Publishing House, Moscow 1953, p. 86. For the Scottish Philosophical Radicals' use of the concept of economic and social class see R. L. Meek, "The Scottish Contribution to Marxist Sociology", in *Democracy and the Labour Movement* (1954), edited by J. Saville.
15 K. Marx and F. Engels, *Manifesto of the Communist Party*, Foreign Languages Publishing House, Moscow 1957, p. 83.
16 Ibid., pp. 84–5.
17 Ibid., p. 51.
18 Ibid., p. 57.
19 Avineri, op. cit., p. 59.

20 *Manifesto of the Communist Party*, pp. 67–8.
21 See, for example, Karl Marx, *Critique of the Gotha Programme* for Marx's defence of the *Manifesto*'s principles against Lassalle.
22 Donald MacRae, "The Bolshevik Ideology", in *Ideology and Society: Papers in Sociology and Politics*, Heinemann, London 1961, pp. 181–97.
23 Karl Marx, Preface to *Capital*, Vol. 1, Foreign Languages Publishing House, Moscow 1965, p. 10.
24 For an early example of Marx's slavish, almost mechanical, use of the economists' rational maximizing model of man, see Marx, "The Wages of Labour", in *Economic and Philosophic Manuscripts of 1844*, Progress Publishers edition, Moscow 1959, pp. 23–36. Here Marx does not question the assumption of the driving force of capitalistic self-interest. He is concerned to show that the implications of this for society have been entirely misunderstood or ignored by Smith and the classical economists. For Marx the implications are the ever-increasing exploitation and wage slavery of the workers, an unhappy society.
25 Shlomo Avineri, op. cit., p. 251.

3/ Typology and Politicization

1 This definition follows one of the alternatives identified by Raymond Williams, *Culture and Society 1780–1950*, Penguin Books, Harmondsworth 1961, p. 16.
2 Various recent historical studies exemplify these different aspects: on labour sectarianism, E. Hobsbawm, *Primitive Rebels*, Manchester University Press, Manchester 1959, pp. 126–45; on socialist intellectual movements, A. M. McBriar, *Fabian Socialism and English Politics*, Cambridge University Press, London 1962; and Margaret Cole, *The Story of Fabian Socialism*, Heinemann, London 1961. The nationalist and ultra-patriotic strand of the early socialism is represented in the writings of Robert Blatchford, and later by George Orwell.
3 See, for example, Alfred Cobban, *The Social Interpretation of the French Revolution*, Cambridge University Press, London 1964.
4 David Truman, "Political Group Analysis", in *International Encyclopedia of the Social Sciences*, Vol. 12, 1968, pp. 241–5.
5 Arthur F. Bentley, *The Process of Government*, University of Chicago Press, 1908, p. 211.
6 Ibid., pp. 258–9.
7 Cf., Mancur Olson, *The Logic of Collective Action*, Harvard University Press, Cambridge, Mass. 1965, for cogent theoretical criticisms on these lines.
8 Robert A. Dahl, *Pluralist Democracy in the United States*, Rand McNally, Chicago 1967, can be placed as a distinguished recent contribution to this tradition.
9 J. G. LaPalombara, *Interest Groups in Italian Politics*, Princeton University Press, Princeton, New Jersey 1964.
10 S. E. Finer, *Anonymous Empire*, Pall Mall Press, London 1958.
11 J. D. Stewart, *British Pressure Groups*, Oxford University Press, London 1958.
12 G. Almond and J. Coleman, *The Politics of Developing Areas*, Princeton University Press, Princeton, New Jersey 1960, chapter 1.
13 Francis G. Castles, *Pressure Groups and Political Culture: A comparative study*, Routledge and Kegan Paul, London 1967, p. 1.
14 Ibid., p. 2.

15 W. J. M. Mackenzie, op. cit., pp. 215–27.
16 For example, S. M. Lipset, *The First New Nation: The United States in Historical and Comparative Perspective*, Heinemann, London 1964, and Barrington Moore, *Social Origins of Democracy and Dictatorship*, Allen Lane The Penguin Press, London 1967.

4/ Religious Movement, Sect, Millenarism

1 The phrase is also the title of Julian Huxley's *Religion Without Revelation*, Thinkers' Library, London 1940.
2 H. J. Blackham, *Religion in a Modern Society*, Constable, London 1966, p. 11.
3 V. Lanternari, *The Religions of the Oppressed*, Mentor Books, New York 1965.
4 S. F. Nadel, *Nupe Religion*, Routledge and Kegan Paul, London 1954, p. 260.
5 *Marx-Engels Gesamtausgabe*, Volume 1, Section I, Part I, p. 607.
6 Ibid.
7 Ibid.
8 Ernst Troeltsch, *The Social Teaching of the Christian Churches*, translation by Olive Wyon, Allen and Unwin, London 1931, p. 39.
9 Ibid., p. 48.
10 H. Gerth and C. Wright Mills (eds), *From Max Weber*, Oxford University Press, London 1946, pp. 267–87.
11 An interesting single volume attempt at a critique of the major ideas is Roland Robertson's *The Sociological Interpretation of Religion*, Blackwell, 1969.
12 Max Weber (edited and introduced by Talcott Parsons), *The Theory of Social and Economic Organization*, The Free Press, Glencoe 1964, pp. 358–9.
13 Ibid., p. 328.
14 Ibid., p. 359.
15 S. N. Eisenstadt (ed.), *Max Weber: On Charisma and Institution Building*, University of Chicago Press, Chicago 1968, p. 254.
16 For example, see Roland Bainton, *Here I Stand: A Life of Martin Luther*, The New American Library, New York 1965.
17 "The General Character of Charisma", in S. N. Eisenstadt (ed.), op. cit., p. 24.
18 Ibid., S. N. Eisenstadt's introduction, p. xl.
19 *Religionssoziologie* (*The Sociology of Religion*) was first published in 1922 by J. C. B. Mohr (Paul Siebeck), English translation, Methuen, London 1965.
20 Weber excepted movements such as the Donatists of Roman Africa, the Taborites and the Russian peasant sectarians. He argued that they turned against the official church because they feared proletarianization and that they reacted by seeking a revolutionary communal development of the land.
21 Max Weber, *The Sociology of Religion*, Methuen, London 1966, pp. 84–5.
22 Ernst Troeltsch, op. cit., p. 44.
23 Bryan Wilson, *Patterns of Sectarianism*, Heinemann, London, p. 26.
24 Karl Marx, *Capital*, Vol. 1, Volksausgabe, 1, pp. 84–5.
25 David Martin, "Towards the elimination of the concept of 'secularization' ", in *Penguin Survey of Social Sciences*, edited by Julius Gould, London 1965; Leslie Paul, "Studies in the Sociology of Religion: The Selwyn Lectures for 1969", in *Colloquium, The Australia and New Zealand Theological Review*, 1969. For a sociological, occasionally rather glib, discussion of the

evidence for secularizing tendencies see Bryan Wilson, *Religion in Secular Society*, Watts and Co., London 1966.

26 Harvey Cox, *The Secular City*, Student Christian Movement Press, London 1965.

27 B. Holas, "Le Proselytisme en Côte d'Ivoire", in *Vitalité Actuelle des Religions Chrétiennes*, Paris 1959.

28 Georges Balandier, *Sociologie actuelle d'Afrique noire*, Presses Universitaires, Paris 1955, brings out the significance and vitality of this phenomenon with brilliant insight.

29 Norman Cohn, *The Pursuit of the Millennium*, Secker and Warburg, London 1957, p. xiii. For a detailed analysis of doctrinal differences and developments, see Walter L. Wakefield and Austin P. Evans (eds), *Heresies of the High Middle Ages*, Columbia University Press, New York 1969.

30 See J. F. C. Harrison, *Robert Owen and the Owenites in Britain and America: The Quest for the New Moral World*, Routledge and Kegan Paul, London 1969.

31 Useful guidance and bibliographies in this field can be found in: "Revitalization Movements", by Anthony Wallace, in *American Anthropologist*, New Series, 58, 1956, pp. 264–81; *Millenial Dreams in Action*, edited by Sylvia Thrupp, Comparative Studies in Society and History, Supplement No. 2, Mouton, The Hague 1962; and "Millenarism", by Yonina Talmon, in *International Encylopedia of the Social Sciences*, Vol. 10, pp. 349–62.

32 James Mooney's classic study, *The Ghost Dance Religion and the Sioux Outbreak of 1890*, has been edited and abridged in a new edition by Anthony Wallace, University of Chicago Press, Chicago 1965.

33 Peter Worsley, *The Trumpet Shall Sound*, London 1957, pp. 238–9.

34 Ibid., pp. 227–8.

35 Vittorio Lanternari, op. cit.

36 Ibid., p. 243.

37 Max Weber, *The Protestant Ethic and the Spirit of Capitalism*, Allen and Unwin, London 1965; R. H. Tawney, *Religion and the Rise of Capitalism* Penguin Books, Harmondsworth 1969.

38 S. N. Eisenstadt, "The Protestant ethic thesis in analytical and comparative context", *Diogenes*, No. 59, 1967, pp. 25–46.

39 Harold Perkin, *The Origins of Modern English Society*, Routledge and Kegan Paul, London 1969.

40 For an excellent collection of historical essays on some of the issues involved see the special issue of *Journal of Contemporary History* on "Church and Politics", Vol. 2, No. 4, 1967.

41 See G. Goyan, "Histoire religieuse", in *Histoire de la Nation Française*, edited by Hanotaux, for an illuminating general account.

42 J. S. Conway, *The Nazi Persecution of the Churches 1933–1945*, London 1968; Gram *et al.*, *The German Resistance to Hitler*, English translation, 1970; Walter Kolarz, *Religion in the Soviet Union*, St Martin's Press, New York 1961; Michael Bourdeaux, *Religious Ferment in Russia: Protestant Opposition to Soviet Religious Policy*, London 1968.

5/ People, Nation, Race and Empire

1 For example, E. J. Hobsbawm's *Primitive Rebels*, Manchester University Press, 1959 (subtitled "Studies in Archaic Forms of Social Movement in the Nineteenth and Twentieth Centuries") deals with peasant risings and city mobs among other phenomena. Similarly, evolutionist assumptions that such movements belong to a pre-modern phase of human development underlie T. A. Critchley's sequence of 'primitive' or aggressive violence,

'reactive violence' and 'progressive violence' (i.e. violence which occurs in the course of programmatic and co-ordinated campaigns for social reform). See T. A. Critchley, *The Conquest of Violence*, Constable, London 1970.

2 E. J. Hobsbawm and George Rudé, *Captain Swing*, Lawrence and Wishart, London 1969, p. 11.

3 A well-known example is Disraeli: 'I repeat . . . that all power is a trust—that we are accountable for its exercise—that from the people, and for the people, all springs, and all must exist!' *Vivian Grey*, Book, VI, ch. 7.

4 For an interesting critique of the major approaches, and a useful bibliography, see Neil J. Smelser, *Theory of Collective Behaviour*, Routledge and Kegan Paul, London 1962.

5 See Sidney Hook, "Ideologies of Violence", in *Encounter*, April 1970, for a cogent presentation of this approach.

6 E. J. Hobsbawm, "The City Mob", in *Primitive Rebels*, op. cit., pp. 113–25.

7 Ibid., p. 114.

8 A. Soboul, "Problèmes du travail en l'an II", *Annales historiques de la Révolution Française*, No. 144, 1956, and *Les sans-culottes parisiens de l'an* II, 1958.

9 George Rudé, *The Crowd in the French Revolution*, 1959, pp. 178 ff.

10 A. Soboul, "Problèmes du travail en l'an II", p. 241.

11 Alfred Cobban, *The Social Interpretation of the French Revolution*, Cambridge University Press, London 1968, pp. 129–30.

12 For example, Lowenthal and Guterman, *Prophets of Deceit, A Study of the Techniques of the American Agitator*, Harper, New York 1949.

13 'Nec audiend; sunt qui solent docere, "Vox populi, vox dei"; cum tumultuositas vulgi semper insaniae proxima est.' Alcuin, *Epistolae*, 166, para. 9.

14 Gustave Le Bon (1841–1932) French social scientist and physician. Main works published in English translation: *The Psychology of Peoples*, Macmillan, New York 1896; *The Crowd*, Ernest Benn, London 1896; *The Psychology of Socialism*, Macmillan, New York 1899; *The Psychology of Revolution*, Putnam, New York 1913; *The World in Revolt*, T. F. Unwin, London 1921.

15 Le Bon, *The Crowd*, 1896, p. 18.

16 Eric Hoffer's *The True Believer, Thoughts on the Nature of Mass Movements*, Harper and Row, 1951, is a recent popular example of the school. Hoffer's preoccupation with paranoia, violence and destruction in mass movement probably derives from his preoccupation with the examples of Nazism and Bolshevism, just as Le Bon was haunted by fears of the French communards. Le Bon, like Hoffer, found a ready audience in times when men were badly shaken by popular tumult and especially anxious over the survival of a stable old order.

17 Hobsbawm and Rudé, op. cit., pp. 15–16.

18 'Social credit' theory was developed originally by Major C. H. Douglas. He advocated, as a means of overcoming what he believed was an inherently insufficient money supply, and to prevent credit control by banks, that the consumer's purchasing power should be augmented by a form of 'national dividend'. He argued that prices, wages, salaries and dividends should be so fixed that the total of incomes equals the total of prices.

19 See Donald L. McMurry, *Coxey's Army. A Study of the Industrial Army Movement of 1894*, Introduction by John D. Hicks, University of Washington Press, 1968, pp. 288–90.

20 Peter Wiles, "A Syndrome, not a Doctrine: some elementary theses on Populism", in *Populism*, edited by Ionescu and Gellner, Weidenfeld and Nicolson, London 1969, pp. 166–79.

21 On the ideas of nationalism useful works include: Elie Kedourie, *Nationalism*, Hutchinson, London 1960; Alfred Cobban, *National Self-Determination*, Methuen, revised edition, 1970; F. O. Hertz, *Nationality in History and Politics*, London 1944; and E. H. Carr, *Nationalism and After*, Papermac, London 1968.

22 Historical surveys of nationalism of value include: H. M. Chadwick, *The Nationalities of Europe and the Growth of National Ideologies*, Cambridge University Press, 1966; Hans Kohn, *The Age of Nationalism*, New York 1962; and L. Snyder, *The Dynamics of Nationalism, Readings in its Meaning and Development*, Princeton 1964.

23 E. Kedourie, op. cit., p. 13.

24 E. H. Carr, *Nationalism and After*, op. cit.

25 See, for example, on the interesting case of Celtic nationalism: Sir Reginald Coupland, *Welsh and Scottish Nationalism*, Collins, London 1954, and H. J. Hanham, *Scottish Nationalism*, Faber, London 1969.

26 For a brief objective account see P. M. Williams and Martin Harrison, *De Gaulle's Republic*, Macmillan, 1960, pp. 33–74.

27 See Juan Comas, *Racial Myths*, UNESCO, 1958.

28 On anti-Semitism see: Hannah Arendt, *The Origins of Totalitarianism*, Allen and Unwin, 3rd British edition, 1967, pp. 3–120; K. S. Pinson (ed.), *Essays on Anti-Semitism*, London 1946; and James Parkes, *An Enemy of the People, anti-Semitism*, Baltimore 1946.

29 On Negro movements see: John Hope Franklin, *From Slavery to Freedom: A History of American Negroes*, New York 1956; W. E. B. Du Bois, *Black Folk, Then and Now*, New York 1939; Louis Filler, *The Crusade against Slavery: 1830–1860*, New York 1960; Bejamin Quarles, *Black Abolitionists*, Oxford University Press, 1969; Langston Hughes, *Fight for Freedom: The Story of the NAACP*, New York 1958; E. Essien-Udom, *The Black Muslims*, Pelican, 1966; Martin Luther King, Jr., *Stride Toward Freedom*, 1958, and *Where Do We Go From Here: Chaos or Community?* 1967; Stokely Carmichael and C. Hamilton, *Black Power*, Jonathan Cape, 1968.

30 For insight into some of the political problems and bitter conflicts that occurred over US Negro 'Back to Africa' projects see Edmund Cronon, *Black Moses*, University of Wisconsin Press, Madison 1962.

31 See C. Eric Lincoln, *The Black Muslims in America*, Boston 1961.

32 Stanley M. Elkins, *Slavery*, Chicago 1959.

33 For recent confirmation of the importance of this influence see Coretta Young, *My Life with Martin Luther King Jr.*, Hodder and Stoughton, London 1970.

34 See, for example: James Parkes, *An Enemy of the People, anti-Semitism*, Baltimore 1946; M. F. Ashley Montagu, *Man's Most Dangerous Myth. The Fallacy of Race*, New York 1942; Ruth Benedict, *Race, Science and Politics*, New York 1941; and L. C. Dunn and T. Dobzhansky, *Heredity, Race and Society*, New York 1950.

35 For valuable general studies of imperialism and imperialist movements see: J. A. Hobson, *Imperialism: A Study*, Allen and Unwin, 1902; A. P. Thornton, *The Imperial Idea and its Enemies*, Macmillan, 1959; R. Kaebner and H. D. Schrutt, *Imperialism—a Political Word, 1840–1960*, Cambridge University Press, 1964; B. Semmel, *Imperialism and Social Reform*, Allen and Unwin, 1960; and H. Brunschwig, *French Colonialism, 1871–1894; Myths and Realities*, Pall Mall Press, 1966. For a classic study of a major pan-movement, see Hans Kohn, *Panslavism, Its History and Ideology*, Notre Dame, Indiana 1953.

6/ Reform and Moral Crusade

1 See Charles Taylor, "Neutrality in Political Science", in *Philosophy, Politics and Society* (Third Series), edited by Peter Laslett and W. G. Runciman, Basil Blackwell, Oxford 1967, pp. 25–57, and Gunar Myrdal, *Objectivity in Social Research*, Duckworth, 1970.

2 For abundant evidence for this see *Essays in Labour History*, edited by Asa Briggs and J. Saville, London 1960.

3 For example, see the meticulous historical analysis of the social and psychological effects of the interwar depression in C. L. Mowat's *Britain Between the Wars 1918–1940*, Methuen, London 1966, pp. 480–531.

4 W. H. Chaloner, "The Agitation Against the Corn Laws", in *Popular Movements c. 1830–1850*, edited by J. T. Ward, Macmillan, London 1970, p. 146.

5 See Peter M. Blau, *Exchange and Power in Social Life*, Wiley, New York 1964, and Frank Parkin, *Middle Class Radicalism*, Manchester University Press, 1968, and the discussion of 'Moral Crusade' and 'Moral Protest', pp. 117–24 of the present work.

6 Werner Sombart, *Socialism and the Social Movement*, Dent, London 1909, p. 8.

7 James Jupp, *Political Parties*, Routledge and Kegan Paul, London 1968, p. 64.

8 R. Tucker, "The Deradicalization of Marxist Movements", in *American Political Science Review*, Vol. LXI, No. 2, June 1967, pp. 343–58.

9 Kenneth Newton, *The Sociology of British Communism*, Allen Lane The Penguin Press, London 1969.

10 Alexis de Tocqueville, *Democracy in America*, World Classics Edition, Oxford University Press, London 1952, pp. 376–7.

11 Ibid., p. 377.

12 Ibid., p. 378.

13 Ibid., pp. 379–80.

14 See, for example, Emile Durkheim, *The Division of Labour*, The Free Press, Glencoe, 2nd edn 1947; Otto von Gierke, *Natural Law and the Theory of Society, 1500–1800*, 2 vols, Cambridge University Press, 1913; F. W. Maitland, "Introduction" to Otto von Gierke's *Political Theories of the Middle Age*, Vol. 3, Cambridge University Press, 1900; J. Neville Figgis, *Churches in the Modern State*, Longmans, London 1913; G. D. H. Cole, *Guild Socialism Restated*, Parsons, London 1920; Harold J. Laski, *A Grammar of Politics*, Yale University Press, New Haven 1925; and Bernard Crick, *In Defence of Politics*, Weidenfeld and Nicolson, London 1962.

15 See, for example, Karl Mannheim, *Ideology and Utopia*, Routledge and Kegan Paul, London 1936; Erich Fromm, *The Fear of Freedom*, Routledge and Kegan Paul, London 1942; Hannah Arendt, *The Burden of our Time*, Secker and Warburg, London 1951; William Kornhauser, *The Politics of Mass Society*, Routledge and Kegan Paul, London 1960.

16 W. Kornhauser, "Mass Society and Mass Phenomena", *International Encyclopaedia of Social Sciences*, Vol. 10, 1968, p. 60.

17 Ibid., p. 60.

18 Ibid., p. 60.

19 S. M. Lipset, M. Trow, J. Coleman, *Union Democracy*, The Free Press, Glencoe 1956, pp. 79–80.

20 I am grateful to my colleague, Dr Ursula Henriques, Department of History, University College, Cardiff, for pointing out to me, as an example of this, the role of the Evangelical-Quaker religionists in promoting penal reform societies and experimental penological projects.

21 On the Chartists, see Mark Hovell, *The Chartist Movement*, Manchester University Press, 1943; Asa Briggs (ed.), *Chartist Studies*, Macmillan, London 1959; A. R. Schoyen, *The Chartist Challenge*, Heinemann, London 1958.

22 Among the few full-length contributions in this area the reader is referred to: Abraham Holtzman, *The Townsend Movement: A Study in Old Age Politics*, Bookman Associates, New York 1963; and Mary R. Dearing, *Veterans in Politics: The Story of the GAR*, Louisiana State University, Baton Rouge 1952.

23 Martin Luther King, *Chaos or Community?* Hodder and Stoughton, London 1968, p. 61.

24 Peter M. Blau, *Exchange and Power in Social Life*, Wiley, New York 1964, pp. 5–6.

25 H. H. Gerth and C. W. Mills (eds), *Max Weber: Essays in Sociology*, Routledge and Kegan Paul, London 1948, p. 120.

26 Frank Parkin, *Middle Class Radicalism*, Manchester University Press, 1968, p. 33.

27 See G. D. H. Cole, *A Short History of the British Working Class Movement 1789–1947*, Allen and Unwin, London, rev. edn 1948, and the biographies of Labour leaders such as Hardie, Henderson, Bevin, Bevan and Fenner Brockway, for supporting evidence.

28 Parkin, op. cit., p. 17.

29 Ibid., pp. 175–92.

30 Gerhard Lenski, "Status Crystallization: A Non-Vertical Dimension of Social Status", *American Sociological Review*, Vol. 19, August 1954.

31 Parkin, op. cit., p. 76.

32 Ibid., p. 77.

33 Ibid., p. 77.

34 Ibid., p. 108.

35 Ibid., p. 109.

36 See S. M. Lipset, "Student Opposition in the US", *Government and Opposition*, Vol. 1, No. 3, 1966, pp. 351–74.

37 See Abrams and A. Little, "The Young Voter in British Politics", *British Journal of Sociology*, Vol. 16, No. 2, 1965, p. 95; and F. Musgrove, *Youth and the Social Order*, Routledge and Kegan Paul, London 1964.

38 Parkin, op. cit., p. 148.

39 See in particular the statement of Leon Jaworski that 'every time a court order is disobeyed, each time an injunction is violated, each occasion on which a court decision is flouted the effectiveness of our judicial system is eroded'. (Quoted in *The Times*, London, December 11, 1969.)

40 See A. Roberts (ed.), *The Strategy of Civilian Defence*, Faber and Faber, London 1967.

41 This picture broadly agrees with the pattern of relations between the British Communist party and CND sketched in Parkin, op. cit., pp. 77–87.

7/ Class and Revolution

1 Harold Perkin, *The Origins of Modern English Society 1780–1880*, Routledge and Kegan Paul, London 1969, p. 17.

2 Ibid., p. 36.

3 E. P. Thompson, *The Making of the English Working Class*, Penguin Books, 1968, p. 212.

4 Perkin, op. cit., p. 37.

5 See on trade unions and labour movements generally: Hugh A. Clegg, Alan

Fox and A. F. Thompson, *A History of British Trade Unions Since 1889*, Clarendon, Oxford 1964; G. D. H. Cole, *A Short History of the British Working-Class Movement 1789–1947* (rev. edn), Allen and Unwin, London 1948; Walter Galenson (ed.), *Comparative Labor Movements*, Prentice-Hall, Englewood Cliffs, New Jersey 1952; Daniel L. Horowitz, *The Italian Labour Movement*, Harvard University Press, 1963; Lewis L. Lorwin, *The International Labor Movements: History, Policies, Outlook*, Harper, New York 1953; Val R. Lorwin, *The French Labor Movement*, Harvard University Press, 1954; Selig Perlman, *The Theory of the Labor Movement*, Kelley, New York 1928; and Sidney and Beatrice Webb, *Industrial Democracy* (rev. edn), Longmans, London 1920.

6 Perkin, op. cit., p. 164.

7 E. Hobsbawm, *Primitive Rebels*, Manchester University Press, 1959, pp. 113 ff. See also A. Mitchell, "The Association Movement of 1792–93", *Historical Journal*, Vol. IV, 1961, pp. 56 ff.

8 E. P. Thompson, op. cit., pp. 19–27.

9 Werner Sombart, *Socialism and The Social Movement* (translation by M. Epstein), Dent, London 1909, p. 137.

10 Ibid., p. 142.

11 Marx, "The Chartists", *New York Daily Tribune*, August 25, 1852.

12 Marx, *Selected Works*, Vol. II, 1942, p. 439.

13 See, for example, regarding Guild Socialists and the origins of the British Communist movement, Walter Kendall, *The Revolutionary Movement in Britain, 1900–1921*, Weidenfeld and Nicolson, London 1969, pp. 278–83.

14 M. Duverger, *Political Parties*, Methuen, London 1964, p. 63.

15 Ibid., p. 63.

16 Ibid., p. 65.

17 J. Blondel, "Mass Parties and Industrialized Societies", *Comparative Government*, edited by J. Blondel, Macmillan, London 1969, pp. 116–26.

18 Ibid., pp. 120–1.

19 Richard Hoggart, *The Uses of Literacy*, Penguin Books, Harmondsworth 1958, p. 5.

20 Ibid., p. 79.

21 Thus, for example, many of W. Kendall's conclusions in *The Revolutionary Movement in Britain, 1900–21*, are vitiated by the failure to take decisive middle-class interventions and élite activities among socialist intellectuals into account in analysing the overall development of the left in Britain both before and during that period.

22 See, for example, K. Newton, *The Sociology of British Communism*, Allen Lane, London 1969, and N. Glazer, *The Social Basis of American Communism*, Harcourt Brace, New York 1961.

23 Lenin, " 'Left-Wing' Communism, An Infantile Disorder", *Selected Works*, Vol. II, Part 2, Moscow 1951, p. 416.

24 Tony Cliff, *The employers' offensive: productivity deals and how to fight them*, Pluto Press, London 1970, p. 230.

25 John Goldthorpe and David Lockwood, "Affluence and the British Class Structure", *Sociological Review*, Vol. XI, No. 2, July 1963.

26 For evidence of Castro's innocence of Marxist-Leninism in the early days of his revolution, see Herbert L. Matthews, *Castro: A Political Biography*, Allen Lane, The Penguin Press, London 1969.

27 E. Hobsbawm, *Primitive Rebels*, Manchester University Press, Manchester 1959, pp. 152 ff.

28 Ibid., p. 162.

29 Quoted in Edmund Wilson's *To the Finland Station*, Fontana, London 1960, p. 279.
30 Lenin, "What Is To Be Done?", in *Selected Works*, Vol. 1, Part 1, Moscow 1950, p. 336.
31 Ibid., pp. 337–8.
32 Philip Selznick, *The Organizational Weapon: A Study of Bolshevik Strategy and Tactics*, Rand Corporation Research Study, New York 1952; see also the authoritative historical study of the CPSU organization, Leonard Schapiro, *The Communist Party of the Soviet Union*, second edition, Methuen, London 1970.
33 Hannah Arendt, *The Burden of our Time*, Secker and Warburg, London 1951, p. 373.
34 See, for example, Carl Friedrich and Zbigniew Brzezinski, *Totalitarian Dictatorship and Autocracy*, Harvard University Press, 1956; and Hannah Arendt, *The Origins of Totalitarianism*, Meridian, New York 1960, which both tend to treat Fascism and Bolshevism as essentially like phenomena.
35 Stokely Carmichael and Charles Hamilton, *Black Power*, Jonathan Cape, London 1968.
36 Ibid., p. 49.
37 Ibid., p. 185.
38 On the general history of anarchist thought, see George Woodcock, *Anarchism*, Penguin Books, Harmondsworth 1968.
39 For some interesting information on Spanish anarchism in relation to Spanish politics, see Gerald Brenan, *The Spanish Labyrinth*, Cambridge University Press, 1943.
40 See H. R. Kedward, *Fascism in Western Europe, 1900–45*, Blackie, London 1969; S. J. Woolf (ed.), *European Fascism*, Weidenfeld and Nicholson, London 1968; F. L. Carsten, *The Rise of Fascism*, Batsford, London 1967; Allen Bullock, *Hitler: A Study in Tyranny*, Odhams, London 1952, also the excellent symposium "International Fascism, 1920–1945", *Journal of Contemporary History*, Vol. 1, No. 1, 1966.
41 Even the Australian leader of the New South Wales, para-military 'New Guard' movement, Eric Campbell, was influenced by Mussolini's method; see Eric Campbell, *The Rallying Point: my story of the New Guard*, Melbourne University Press, 1965.
42 See Adrian Lyttleton, "Fascism in Italy: The Second Wave", *Journal of Contemporary History*, Vol. 1, No. 1, 1966, pp. 75–100, for a careful examination of this evidence.
43 For a recent account of the history of the SS *razzia* of the Roman Jews (1943) and the background to the Italian persecution, see Robert Katz, *Black Sabbath*, Arthur Barker, London 1969.
44 Karl D. Bracher, *Die deutsche Diktatur*, Kiepenheuer and Witsch, Berlin 1969.
45 Marianne Sinclair's report on a visit to North Korea, *The Observer*, November 30, 1969.
46 R. Tucker, "Deradicalization of Marxist Movements", *American Political Science Review*, Vol. LXI, No. 2, June 1967, pp. 343–58.

Conclusion: Moral Dilemmas of Social Movement

1 R. Heberle, *Social Movements: An Introduction to Political Sociology*, Appleton-Century-Crofts Inc., New York 1951, p. 456.

Bibliography

ALMOND, GABRIEL and COLEMAN, JAMES, *The Politics of the Developing Areas*, Princeton University Press, Princeton, New Jersey 1960.

ARENDT, HANNAH, *The Burden of Our Time*, Secker and Warburg, London 1951.

——— *The Origins of Totalitarianism*, Allen and Unwin, London, 3rd British edn 1967.

AVINERI, SHLOMO, *The Social and Political Thought of Karl Marx*, Cambridge University Press, London 1968.

BAINTON, ROLAND, *Here I Stand: A Life of Martin Luther*, The New American Library, New York 1965.

BALANDIER, GEORGES, *Sociologie actuelle d'Afrique noire*, Presses Universitaires, Paris 1955.

BENEDICT, RUTH, *Race, Science, and Politics*, Modern Age Books, New York 1940.

BENTLEY, ARTHUR F., *The Process of Government*, University of Chicago Press, Chicago 1908.

BERLIN, ISAIAH, *Karl Marx*, Oxford University Press, London 1960.

BLACKHAM, H. J., *Religion in a Modern Society*, Constable, London 1966.

BLAU, PETER M., *Exchange and Power in Social Life*, Wiley, New York 1964.

BLONDEL, JEAN, "Mass Parties and Industrialized Societies", in *Comparative Government: A Reader*, edited by Jean Blondel, Macmillan, London 1969.

BLUMER, HERBERT, "Collective Behaviour", in *Review of Sociology: Analysis of a Decade*, edited by Gittler, Wiley, New York 1957.

BOURDEAUX, MICHAEL, *Religious Ferment in Russia: Protestant opposition to Soviet Religious Policy*, Macmillan, London 1968.

BRACHER, KARL D., *Die deutsche Diktatur*, Kiepenheuer and Witsch, Berlin 1969.

BRENAN, GERALD, *The Spanish Labyrinth*, Cambridge University Press, London 1943.

BRIGGS, ASA (ed.), *Chartist Studies*, Macmillan, London 1959.

BRIGGS, ASA and SAVILLE, J. (eds), *Essays in Labour History*, London 1960.

BRUNSCHWIG, H., *French Colonialism, 1871–1894, Myths and Realities*, Pall Mall Press, London 1966.

BULLOCK, ALAN, *Hitler: A Study in Tyranny*, Odhams, London 1952.

CAMPBELL, ERIC, *The Rallying Point: my story of the New Guard*, Melbourne University Press, Melbourne 1965.

CARMICHAEL, STOKELY and HAMILTON, CHARLES, *Black Power*, Jonathan Cape, London 1968.

CARR, E. H., *Nationalism and After*, Papermac Edition, London 1968.

——— *What is History?*, Penguin Books, Harmondsworth, Middlesex 1964.

CARSTEN, F. L., *The Rise of Fascism*, Batsford, London 1967.

CASTLES, FRANCIS G., *Pressure Groups and Political Culture: A Comparative Study*, Routledge and Kegan Paul, London 1967.

CHADWICK, H. M., *The Nationalities of Europe and the Growth of National Ideologies*, Cambridge University Press, London 1966.

Clegg, Hugh A., Fox, Alan and Thompson, A. F., *A History of British Trade Unions since 1889*, Clarendon, Oxford 1964.

Cliff, Tony, *The Employers' Offensive: Productivity Deals and How to Fight Them*, Pluto Press, London 1970.

Cobban, Alfred, *National Self-Determination*, Methuen, London, new edn 1970.

——— *The Social Interpretation of the French Revolution*, London 1964.

Cohn, Norman, *The Pursuit of the Millennium*, Secker and Warburg, London 1957.

Cole, G. D. H., *Guild Socialism Restated*, Parsons, London 1920.

——— *A Short History of the British Working Class Movement 1789–1947*, Allen and Unwin, London, rev. edn 1948.

Cole, Margaret, *The Story of Fabian Socialism*, Heinemann, London 1961.

Comas, Juan, *Racial Myths*, UNESCO, 1958.

Coupland, Sir Reginald, *Welsh and Scottish Nationalism*, Collins, London 1954.

Cox, Harvey, *The Secular City*, Student Christian Movement Press, London 1965.

Crick, Bernard, *In Defence of Politics*, Weidenfeld and Nicolson, London 1962.

Cronon, Edmund, *Black Moses*, University of Wisconsin Press, Madison 1962.

Dahl, Robert A., *Pluralist Democracy in the United States*, Rand McNally, Chicago 1967.

Dearing, Mary R., *Veterans in Politics: The Story of the GAR*, Louisiana State University, Baton Rouge 1952.

Dubois, W. E. B., *Black Folk, Then and Now. An Essay in the history and sociology of the Negro Race*, H. Holt and Co., New York 1940.

Dunn, L. C. and Dobzhansky, T., *Heredity, Race and Society*, Mentor Books, New York 1946.

Durkheim, Émile, *The Division of Labour*, The Free Press, Glencoe, Ill., 2nd edn 1947.

Duverger, M., *Political Parties*, Methuen, London 1964.

Eisenstadt, S. N. (ed.), *Max Weber: On Charisma and Institution Building*, Chicago University Press, Chicago 1968.

Elkins, Stanley M., *Slavery*, Chicago University Press, Chicago 1959.

Engels, Friedrich, *The Conditions of the Working Class in England* (1st published in German 1845), 1st English edn 1892, Panther Books edition with introduction by E. Hobsbawm, London 1969.

Essien-Udom, E., *The Black Muslims*, Penguin Books, Harmondsworth, Middlesex 1966.

Etzioni, A., *A Comparative Analysis of Complex Organizations*, The Free Press, Glencoe, Ill. 1961.

Figgis, J. Neville, *Churches in the Modern State*, Longmans, London 1913.

Filler, Louis, *The Crusade against Slavery: 1830–1860*, Harper and Row, New York 1960.

Finer, S. E., *Anonymous Empire*, Pall Mall Press, London 1958.

Franklin, John Hope, *From Slavery to Freedom: A History of American Negroes*, Afred A. Knopf, New York 1948.

Friedrich, Carl and Brzezinski, Zbigniew, *Totalitarian Dictatorship and Autocracy*, Harvard University Press, Cambridge, Mass. 1956.

Fromm, Erich, *The Fear of Freedom*, Routledge and Kegan Paul, London 1942.

Galenson, Walter (ed.), *Comparative Labor Movements*, Prentice-Hall, Englewood Cliffs, New Jersey 1952.

Gerth, H. and Mills, C. Wright (eds), *From Max Weber*, Oxford University Press, London 1946.

——— *Max Weber: Essays in Sociology*, Routledge and Kegan Paul, London 1948.

GIERKE, OTTO VON, *Natural Law and the Theory of Society, 1500–1800*, 2 vols, Cambridge University Press, London 1913.

GLAZER, N., *The Social Basis of American Communism*, Harcourt Brace, New York 1961.

GOLDTHORPE, JOHN and LOCKWOOD, DAVID, "Affluence and the British Class Structure", *Sociological Review*, Vol. XI, No. 2, July 1963.

HANHAM, H. J., *Scottish Nationalism*, Faber, London 1969.

HANOTAUX, G. (ed.), *Histoire de la nation Française*, Paris 1921.

HARRISON, J. F. C., *Robert Owen and the Owenites in Britain and America: The Quest for the New Moral World*, Routledge and Kegan Paul, London 1996.

HEBERLE, RUDOLF, *Social Movements: An Introduction to Political Sociology*, Appleton-Century-Crofts Inc., New York 1951.

——— "Types and Functions of Social Movements", in *International Encyclopaedia of the Social Sciences*, Collier Macmillan, New York 1968, pp. 438–44.

HERTZ, F. O., *Nationality in History and Politics*, London 1944.

HOBSBAWM, ERIC, *Primitive Rebels*, Manchester University Press, Manchester 1959.

HOBSBAWM, ERIC and RUDÉ, GEORGE, *Captain Swing*, Lawrence and Wishart, London 1969.

HOBSON, J. A., *Imperialism: A Study*, Allen and Unwin, London 1902.

HOFFER, ERIC, *The True Believer*, Harper and Row, New York 1951.

HOGGART, RICHARD, *The Uses of Literacy*, Penguin Books, Harmondsworth, Middlesex 1958.

HOLTZMAN, ABRAHAM, *The Townsend Movement: A Study in Old Age Politics*, Bookman Associates, New York 1963.

HOOK, SIDNEY, *Marx and the Marxists: The Ambiguous Legacy*, Princeton University Press, Princeton, New Jersey 1955.

HOROWITZ, DANIEL L., *The Italian Labour Movement*, Harvard University Press, Cambridge, Mass. 1963.

HOVELL, MARK, *The Chartist Movement*, Manchester University Press, Manchester 1943.

HUGHES, LANGSTON, *Fight for Freedom: The Story of the NAACP*, New York 1958.

HUXLEY, JULIAN, *Religion Without Revelation*, Thinkers' Library, London 1940.

IONESCU, GHITA and GELLNER, ERNEST (eds), *Populism: its meanings and national characteristics*, Weidenfeld and Nicolson, London 1969.

JUPP, JAMES, *Political Parties*, Routledge and Kegan Paul, London 1968.

KAEBNER, R. and SCHRUTT, H. D., *Imperialism—a Political Word, 1840–1960*, Cambridge University Press, London 1964.

KATZ, ROBERT, *Black Sabbath*, Arthur Barker, London 1969.

KEDOURIE, E., *Nationalism*, Hutchinson, London 1960.

KEDWARD, H. R., *Fascism in Western Europe, 1900–45*, Blackie, London 1969.

KENDALL, WALTER, *The Revolutionary Movement in Britain, 1900–1921*, Weidenfeld and Nicolson, London 1969.

KING, MARTIN LUTHER, *Chaos or Community?*, Hodder and Stoughton, London 1968.

KOHN, HANS, *The Idea of Nationalism. A Study in its origins and background*, Macmillan and Co., New York 1945.

——— *Panslavism, Its History and Ideology*, Notre Dame, South Bend, Indiana 1953.

KOLARZ, WALTER, *Religion in the Soviet Union*, St Martin's Press, New York 1961.

KORNHAUSER, WILLIAM, "Mass Society and Mass Phenomena", in *International Encyclopedia of Social Sciences*, Vol. 10, Collier Macmillan, 1968, pp. 58–64.

——— *The Politics of Mass Society*, Routledge and Kegan Paul, London 1960.

LANTERNARI, V., *The Religions of the Oppressed*, Mentor Books, New York 1965.

LAPALOMBARA, J. G., *Interest Groups in Italian Politics*, Princeton University Press, Princeton, New Jersey 1964.

LASKI, HAROLD J., *A Grammar of Politics*, Yale University Press, New Haven 1925.

LE BON, GUSTAVE, *The Crowd*, Ernest Benn, London 1896.

——— *The Psychology of Peoples*, Macmillan, New York 1896.

——— *The Psychology of Socialism*, Macmillan, New York, 1899.

——— *The Psychology of Revolution*, Putnam, New York 1913.

——— *The World in Revolt*, T. F. Unwin, London 1921.

LENIN, V., " 'Left-Wing' Communism, An Infantile Disorder", in *Selected Works*, Vol. 11, Part 2, Moscow 1951.

——— "What Is To Be Done?", in *Selected Works*, Vol. 1, Part 1, Moscow 1950.

LINCOLN, C. ERIC, *The Black Muslims in America*, Boston 1961.

LIPSET, S. M., TROW, MARTIN A. and COLEMAN, JAMES S., *Union Democracy*, The Free Press. Glencoe, Ill. 1956.

LIPSET, S. M., *The First New Nation: The United States in Historical and Comparative Perspective*, Heinemann, London 1964.

——— "Student Opposition in the US", *Government and Opposition*, Vol. 1, No. 3, 1966, pp. 351–74.

LOCKE, HUME, ROUSSEAU, *Social Contract*, World Classics Edition, Oxford University Press, London 1947.

LORWIN, LEWIS L., *The International Labour Movements: History, Policies, Outlook*, Harper, New York 1953.

LORWIN, VAL. R., *The French Labor Movement*, Harvard University Press, Cambridge, Mass. 1954.

LOWENTHAL and GUTERMAN, *Prophets of Deceit, A Study of the Techniques of the American Agitator*, Harper, New York 1949.

MCBRIAR, A. M., *Fabian Socialism and English Politics*, Cambridge University Press, London 1962.

MACKENZIE, W. J. M., *Politics and Social Science*, Penguin Books, Harmondsworth, Middlesex 1967.

MCMURRY, DONALD L., *Coxey's Army. A Study of the Industrial Army Movement of 1894*, Introduction by John D. Hicks, University of Washington Press, 1968.

MACRAE, DONALD, *Ideology and Society: Papers in Sociology and Politics*, Heinemann, London 1961.

MAITLAND, F. W., "Introduction", in *Political Theories of the Middle Age*, Vol. 3, by Otto von Gierke, Cambridge University Press, London 1900.

MANNHEIM, KARL, *Ideology and Utopia*, Routledge and Kegan Paul, London 1936.

MARTIN, DAVID, "Towards the elimination of the concept of secularization", in *Penguin Survey of Social Sciences*, edited by Julius Gould, Penguin Books Harmondsworth, Middlesex 1965.

MARX, KARL, *Capital* (1st English edn 1886), Progress Publishers, Moscow 1965.

——— *Economic and Philosophic Manuscripts of 1844*, Progress Publishers, Moscow 1959.

MARX, KARL and ENGELS, FRIEDRICH, *The Communist Manifesto*, Foreign Languages Publishing House, Moscow 1957.

—— *Selected Correspondence*, Foreign Languages Publishing House, Moscow 1953.

MATTHEWS, HERBERT, *Castro: A Political Biography*, Allen Lane, London 1969.

MONTAGU, M. F. ASHLEY, *Man's Most Dangerous Myth: the Fallacy of Race*, Harper and Bros, New York 1952.

MOONEY, JAMES, *The Ghost-Dance Religion and the Sioux Outbreak of 1890*, abridged, with an introduction by Anthony F. C. Wallace, University of Chicago Press, Chicago 1965.

MOORE, BARRINGTON, *Social Origins of Democracy and Dictatorship*, Allen Lane, the Penguin Press, London 1967.

MOWAT, C. L., *Britain Between the Wars 1918–1940*, Methuen, London 1966.

MUSGROVE, F., *Youth and the Social Order*, Routledge and Kegan Paul, London 1964.

MYRDAL, GUNAR, *Objectivity in Social Research*, Duckworth, London 1970.

NADEL, S. F., *Nupe Religion*, Routledge and Kegan Paul, London 1954.

NEWTON, KENNETH, *The Sociology of British Communism*, Allen Lane The Penguin Press, London 1969.

NIEHBUHR, H. RICHARD, *The Social Sources of Denominationalism*, first published 1929, Harper, New York 1957.

OLSON, MANCUR, *The Logic of Collective Action: Public Goods and the Theory of Groups*, Harvard University Press, Cambridge, Mass. 1965.

PARKES, JAMES, *An Enemy of the People, anti-Semitism*, Penguin Books, Baltimore 1946.

PARKIN, FRANK, *Middle Class Radicalism: The Social Bases of the British Campaign for Nuclear Disarmament*, Manchester University Press, Manchester 1968.

PAUL, LESLIE, "Studies in the Sociology of Religion. The Selwyn Lectures for 1969", in *Colloquium. The Australia and New Zealand Theological Review*, 1969.

PERKIN, HAROLD, *The Origins of Modern English Society*, Routledge and Kegan Paul, London 1969.

PERLMAN, SELIG, *The Theory of the Labor Movement*, Kelley, New York 1928.

POPE, LISTON, *Millhands and Preachers: A Study of Gastonia*, Yale University Press, New York 1942.

QUARLES, BENJAMIN, *Black Abolitionists*, Oxford University Press, New York 1969.

REES, JOHN C., "Lenin and Marxism", in *Lenin: the Man, the Theorist, the Leader*, edited by L. Schapiro and P. Reddaway, Pall Mall Press, London 1967.

RICHMOND, A. H., "The Sociology of Migration", in *Migration*, edited by J. A. Jackson, Cambridge University Press, London 1970.

ROBERTS, A. (ed.), *The Strategy of Civilian Defence*, Faber and Faber, London 1967.

ROBERTSON, ROLAND, *The Sociological Interpretation of Religion*, Blackwell, Oxford 1969.

RUDÉ, GEORGE, *The Crowd in the French Revolution*, Clarendon Press, London 1959.

SCHAPIRO, LEONARD, *The Communist Party of the Soviet Union*, second edition, Methuen, London 1970.

SCHOYEN, A. R., *The Chartist Challenge*, Heinemann, London 1958.

SCHUMPETER, J. A., *Capitalism, Socialism and Democracy*, Harper, New York 1942.

SELZNICK, PHILIP, *The Organizational Weapon. A Study of Bolshevik Strategy and Tactics*, Rand Corporation Research Study, New York 1952.

SEMMEL, B., *Imperialism and Social Reform*, Allen and Unwin, London 1960.
SEYMOUR CONWAY, JOHN, *The Nazi Persecution of the Churches 1933–45*, Weidenfeld and Nicolson, London 1968.
SMELSER, NEIL, *Theory of Collective Behaviour*, Routledge and Kegan Paul, London 1962.
SNYDER, L., *The Dynamics of Nationalism, Readings in its Meaning and Development*, Princeton University Press, Princeton, New Jersey 1964.
SOBOUL, A., *The Parisian Sansculottes and the French Revolution 1793–4*, English translation by Gwynne Lewis, Clarendon Press, London 1964.
SOMBART, WERNER, *Socialism and the Social Movement*, first English translation, Dent, London 1909.
SOREL, GEORGE, *Reflections on Violence*, translation by T. E. Hulme and J. Roth, with an introduction by Edward A. Shils, Collier Books, New York 1961.
STARK, WERNER, *The Sociology of Religion: A Study of Christendom*, Vol. 4, Routledge and Kegan Paul, London 1969.
STEIN, LORENZ VON, *The History of the Social Movement in France 1789–1850*, edited and translated by Dr K. Mengelberg, Bedminster Press, Totowa, New Jersey 1964.
STEWART, J. D., *British Pressure Groups*, Oxford University Press, London 1958.
TALMON, J. L., *The Origins of Totalitarian Democracy*, Secker and Warburg, London 1952.
TALMON, YONINA, "Millenarism", in *International Encyclopaedia of the Social Sciences*, Vol. 10, Collier Macmillan, New York 1968, pp. 349–62.
TAWNEY, R. H., *Religion and the Rise of Capitalism*, Penguin Books, Harmondsworth, Middlesex 1969.
TAYLOR, CHARLES, "Neutrality in Political Science", in *Philosophy, Politics and Society* (third series), edited by Peter Laslett and W. G. Runciman, Basil Blackwell, Oxford 1967.
THOMPSON, E. P., *The Making of the English Working Class*, Penguin Books, Harmondsworth, Middlesex 1968.
THORNTON, A. P., *The Imperial Idea and its Enemies*, Macmillan, London 1959.
THRUPP, SYLVIA (ed.), *Millenial Dreams in Action*, Comparative Studies in Society and History, Supplement No. 2, Mouton, The Hague 1962.
TOCQUEVILLE, ALEXIS DE, *Democracy in America*, World Classics Edition, Oxford University Press, London 1952.
TÖNNIES, FERDINAND, *Community and Association*, Routledge and Kegan Paul, London 1955.
TROELTSCH, ERNST, *The Social Teachings of the Christian Churches*, English translation by Olive Wyon, Allen and Unwin, London 1931.
TRUMAN, DAVID, "Political Group Analysis", in *International Encyclopaedia of the Social Sciences*, Vol. 12, Collier Macmillan, New York 1968, pp. 241–5.
TUCKER, R., "Deradicalization of Marxist Movements", *American Political Science Review*, Vol. LXI, No. 2, June 1967, pp. 343–58.
VAN BUREN, PAUL, *The Secular Meaning of the Gospel, based on an analysis of its language*, Student Christian Movement Press, London 1963.
WAKEFIELD, WALTER L. and EVANS, AUSTIN P. (eds), *Heresies of the High Middle Ages*, Columbia University Press, New York 1969.
WALLACE, ANTHONY, "Mass Phenomena", in *International Encyclopaedia of the Social Sciences*, Vol. 10, Collier Macmillan, New York 1968, pp. 54–8.
——— "Revitalization Movements", in *American Anthropologist*, New Series, 58, 1956, pp. 264–81.
WEBB, SIDNEY and BEATRICE, *Industrial Democracy*, Longmans, London, rev. edn 1920.

WEBER, MAX, *The Protestant Ethic and the Spirit of Capitalism*, Allen and Unwin, London 1965.

——— *The Sociology of Religion*, Methuen, London 1965.

——— *The Theory of Social and Economic Organization*, edited and introduced by Talcott Parsons, The Free Press, Glencoe, Ill. 1964.

WELDON, T. D., *The Vocabulary of Politics*, Penguin Books, Harmondsworth, Middlesex 1955.

WILLIAMS, P. M. and HARRISON, M., *De Gaulle's Republic*, Macmillan, London 1960.

WILLIAMS, RAYMOND, *Culture and Society 1750–1950*, Penguin Books, Harmondsworth, Middlesex 1961.

WILSON, BRYAN, *Patterns of Sectarianism: Organization and Ideology in Social and Religious Movements*, Heinemann, London 1967.

——— *Religion in Secular Society*, Watts and Co., London 1966.

WILSON, EDMUND, *To The Finland Station*, Fontana, London 1960.

WOLFE, BERTRAM D., *Marxism: One Hundred Years in the Life of a Doctrine*, Chapman and Hall, London 1967.

WOODCOCK, GEORGE, *Anarchism*, Penguin Books, Harmondsworth, Middlesex 1967.

WOOLF, S. J. (ed.), *European Fascism*, Weidenfeld and Nicolson, London 1968.

WORSLEY, PETER, *The Trumpet Shall Sound: a Study of 'cargo' cults in Melanesia*, MacGibbon and Kee, London 1957.

YOUNG, CORETTA, *My Life with Martin Luther King Jnr.*, Hodder and Stoughton, London 1970.

YOUNG, MICHAEL, *The Rise of the Meritocracy 1870–2033: an essay on education and equality*, Thames and Hudson, London 1958.

Index